ON THE OUTSIDE LOOKING IN

ONE MOTHER'S JOURNAL OF HER FAMILY'S BATTLE WITH A MOOD DISORDER

Jody M. Ehrhardt

PublishAmerica
Baltimore

First printing

ISBN: 1-4137-2266-0
PUBLISHED BY PUBLISHAMERICA, LLLP
www.publishamerica.com
Baltimore

Printed in the United States of America

This book is dedicated to my son, Xanthe, and my daughter, Jahni, who, with their love, innocence, imagination, intelligence and wonderful smiles, make each day better than the last.

Acknowledgments

In keeping with the pattern of first books, which renders the acknowledgment page almost as long as the book itself, I plan to thank everyone who has ever helped me with anything.

First, I would like to thank my children, Xanthe and Tahni, for letting me share their life stories and for putting up with the hours that I spent glued to the computer. I also want to thank them for the valuable life lessons they have taught me and for their undying, unconditional love. You two are my reason for living. I love you both.

I would like to thank my fiancé, Chris, for loving me, believing in me and supporting me through the writing of this book. I love you.

I want to thank my mom for everything. For raising me with love, for supporting me, for being my rock when I couldn't stand on my own, for helping me raise my kids, for loving me unselfishly, for being my mom. You are a beautiful person. I love you.

I want to thank my dad, who passed away in 1995, for pushing me to be the best I could be, for believing in me, for giving me the skills to succeed and for loving me. I love you and miss you terribly.

I want to thank my ex-husband for continuing to be so present in our children's lives, for relieving me by taking the kids when I needed a break and for trusting me and backing me up in all of my ventures in securing treatment for our son.

I want to thank my sister for her enormous amount of help in the early years and for letting me vent during the last few months.

I want to thank Roger for supporting me, believing in me and listening to me for hours when I was down. Any girl would be lucky to have you as a dad, thanks for stepping in.

I want to thank my (soon to be) mother-in-law, father-in-law and two sisters-in-law for trying so hard to understand my craziness and accepting me, problems and all.

I want to thank Karen Fitzgerald, Monica Powell and Janiece Larkin for listening to me, supporting me and for being my friends.

Lastly, I want to thank Publish America for believing in me and my book and my editor for walking me through the publishing process.

Foreword

    My decision to write, and then publish this book, was a very complicated and personal one. What started out as a simple way to work through my frustration and fear, turned out to be a very descriptive picture of our lives. A journey of our ups and downs as we fought my son's mental illness and tried to cope as a family. As I reread the entries, I realized that many families must be going through a lot of the same things that we were. Like me, they must feel alone, confused and isolated. My biggest questions have always been... Will this ever get better? and How does everyone else live through this? In order to share our story, I realized that I would have to open our lives up to the scrutiny of the world. I decided that it would be worth it if our story could help even one other family to get through their pain. If nothing else, maybe we could let them know they were not alone.

    As our years of suffering went by, I began to learn more about anxiety and mood disorders and I met a few other families like ours. As we started talking, the same concerns kept being voiced over and over again. Why is getting help for our children almost as hard as living with the illness itself? Why do we have to dig for information in order to educate those that should be educating us? How can the "professionals" send us home after one hour of therapy knowing that we still do not have the tools necessary to live through the next 6 days and 23 hours? How can they stand to see us beg for help and cry in frustration and not try harder to get us the information we so desperately need? Most importantly, how can any of this be allowed to happen and why do so many families have to suffer needless? As one child put it... What do I have to tell these doctors to get them to help me? How sick do I have to be? If I told them I was going to kill you, would they help me then? Because of all of these questions, I have included a short synopsis at the end of this book that outlines concrete resources and treatments, that I think every family should look into. Somehow in our fight for help, we managed to go without these important components for more than 10 years. If I had known about these things earlier, I feel that we could have avoided most or at least some of our struggles. I list them here so that maybe other families can avoid wasted years of pain by knowing what to ask for from the start.

OUR BACKGROUND

From birth on, I always knew my son was different from other kids. He required very little sleep, he was extremely smart, easily frustrated and all over the map, emotion wise. I have always been an extremely sensitive person, so I chalked it up to his personality. But as I look back now, I can see that I have always tried to protect him. I never wanted anyone else to see him as different. I also related to him in a slightly different manner. It's as if I knew somehow that he saw the world a little differently, and that he would at times need protection from the real world, and also from the world in his mind.

My son did not sleep all night until the age of 5 (and then for the next seven years he had more rough nights than restful ones). Every night he would wake up at least 4 times, sometimes as many as 20 times, crying out for me. He always had bad dreams. I spent the majority of my nights sleeping in his room or taking him into mine. My husband, at the time, worked nights so this wasn't as big of problem as it could have been. But we did of course argue about his sleeping habits. When I tried to tell people about his problems with sleeping, they just told me to be tougher with him or chalked it up to him being spoiled. But they didn't see him at night. They did not see the raw fear in his eyes. I did try to be tough though. For a month I tried to put Xanthe in his own bed and make him stay there. He wouldn't just cry for thirty minutes or an hour. He would cry all night until as the sun was coming up we would give in and bring him into our bed. Once there he would instantly drift off to sleep.

Some nights I would lie down with him in his bed until he fell asleep then I would sneak off to my own room. He would wake up so many times throughout the night though that eventually I would just stay in his room or I would bring him back into mine. The first time that he slept through the night I ran into his room around 2am thinking he had died in his sleep. I even went as far as to put a mirror in front of his nose to reassure myself that he was still breathing! By this time my body had been trained to wake up at night and when he didn't wake with me I feared the worst.

Xanthe was also a very picky child. Not a spoiled kind of picky, but an uncomfortable with things kind of picky. Many times he would refuse to eat his favorite food because it looked or smelled funny. We also had a huge problem with socks. They never felt right. They always hurt his feet. My mother and I searched the world over for a brand of socks that he could wear. We tried every brand out there, both inside out and outside out. Nothing worked. We even tried having him wear no socks at all. That just caused his feet to hurt worse. Mom and I would laugh about the crazy things we were reduced to doing, but she always did them with me and she never judged. Others though, again, chalked it up to him being spoiled. At times I believed them, but at other times I saw the real discomfort these things were causing him. I never understood them, but I knew these feelings were real.

Xanthe was also extremely intelligent. At the age of six months he knew his colors. We would show him off to our friends like he was some kind of circus trick. We would have our friends line up colored balls in whatever order they chose then tell Xanthe to pick a certain color. He always picked correctly.

He could also come up with very abstract thoughts and reasonings at an early age. His ideas for new inventions amazed people with their detail and well-planned mechanics. He was always coming up with new ideas to start a business with, and get rich! I have eaten a strange spaghetti sauce that he invented that contained chocolate sauce, a soup made from grass and weeds and some tree bark that had been flavored with cinnamon and sugar. The tree bark actually wasn't that bad, and he did manage to sell some to his friends.

His best business idea came about when he was five years old. He saw a bag of individually wrapped chocolates sitting on the counter. He asked me if he could have them. I thought he meant a few and said yes. A little while later he came in from outside and his fists were full of money. We were living with my mom at the time, in the neighborhood I grew up in, so everyone knew everyone on our block.

It turns out that Xanthe had taken that bag of candy and went door to door selling each piece for a dollar. Of course everyone knew him, but his biggest selling point was his personality. People used to tease him by saying that he could sell ice to Eskimos if he wanted to. When I found out what he had done I took him back around the neighborhood and tried to return the money. No one would take it back. Most refused to take their money back because they thought he was cute, but other's felt that he deserved it for coming up with the plan in the first place!

Unfortunately, along with this intelligence came an abnormal talent for coming up with fears that most kids didn't think much about. He was afraid of burglars mostly, but also of fire or other "accidents." One day, when he had been playing in the front yard, he came inside screaming with fear. Come to find out he had memorized all of the cars that belonged on our block and he saw a "strange" car drive by twice, so he decided that it was coming by to kill him. It took a week to get him to go back outside. I remember thinking at the time that it must be so hard for him to play like a regular kid if he had to first memorize his surrounding to relax and have fun. I cried for his loss of a carefree, innocent childhood. His fears were always well thought out like adult fears ,only he lacked the maturity to know that these things, while probable ,were more likely improbable. He had adult intelligence, but lacked adult reason. This can be a very scary combination.

Xanthe also talked very early. By the time he was 18 months old he was talking in complete clear sentences. When he was 12 months old he would walk into my room in the middle of the night and state plainly that he was scared. I would freak out; I am ashamed to say this, but it scared me. Here was this little baby walking and talking like an adult, standing by my bed. It always made me think of that horror movie *Chucky*.

Even with these problems everyone loved him. He was outgoing, funny, smart and very articulate. He could talk all day long. He has always been a talker. The only outward "flaw" in his personality at this point was that he suffered from exaggerated separation anxiety.

By the time most kids were separating from their mothers, mine was closing in. We had a heck of a time sending him to preschool. Kindergarten, first grade and second grade were the same way. Everyone told me it was because I spoiled him. He was a mommy's boy. But I knew something else was wrong. He wasn't just afraid to leave me because it was different for him, he was afraid to leave me because he was convinced one of us would be killed before school got out.

By the middle of second grade it all came to a head. Things were getting worse. He couldn't even start bedtime in his own room. He was afraid of unrealistic things. One night he thought his bed was filling up with sand. Another night he was convinced that a burglar was waiting (for hours?) to come upstairs to kill him when I left. We tried some very creative ways to deal with all of this. I spent one night shoveling pretend sand from his bed. Another night I helped him build a burglar trap at his door. I once even strung the staircase with fishing line so that it would trip the burglar if he tried to sneak up at night. Of course, the next morning I am the one that tripped over the string and fell down the stairs!

School attendance was also getting worse. He was afraid that if I left him, I would never return. It got so bad at one point that the principal had to meet me at the car every morning and pry Xanthe, screaming and crying, from my body and drag him into school.

This, of course, broke my heart and I cried all the way to work, but everyone assured me we were doing the right thing. I might have believed them if things had gotten better after a few weeks, but instead they got worse. And months later we were still following the same routine. Only now the school had decided that I shouldn't be the one dropping him off. They thought I was making his anxiety worse. I didn't want to put the burden of all of this on someone else, but I wanted to do anything I could to help Xanthe. So I enlisted the help of my mom and sister. They each spent two weeks taking Xanthe to school. They both had to endure the crying and begging. The principal had to pry him away from them also. It also made each of them cry. It got to a point where, as they drove away, they were becoming physically ill with the anguish of what they had just done. My sister was funny though. I can not count how many times she would call me at work at 8:30 to inform me that she just couldn't go through with it and had taken Xanthe home with her. I will always be grateful to both of them for what they tried to do. Xanthe was lucky in that respect. Both of my kids were. They didn't just have one mom all those years, they had three. My mom and sister loved them, sacrificed for them and treated them just like they were their own kids.

Around this same time, night time became unbearable. We would sit in the bathroom together all night, every night. I would lean against the wall and he would sit between my legs. I would wrap my arms around him and try to take his pain away. He would cry and shake and throw up. In between all of this, he would beg me not to leave him; not to make him go. I have to admit that many times I gave in and called him in sick to school. I also called his sister, Tahni, in. She would be so tired from lack of sleep, that she could barely hold her eyes open. She was in kindergarten at the time and sometimes she could be so grown up and funny. One night after hours of listening to Xanthe and me in the bathroom, she staggered down the hall, exhausted, and clutching her baby blanket. "Can you two please be quiet? I have to go to school tomorrow," she begged between yawns. If it had happened under any other circumstances I would have laughed. Instead it made me cry.

There is no way to convey the emotion of those long nights. He wasn't just crying, he was experiencing pure terror. His eyes scared me the most. His pupils were always abnormally dilated and his eyes kept darting around the room in fear. His screams ran a close second. They were filled with so much emotion and fear that listening to them gave me goose bumps. I felt completely helpless. I also felt like a complete failure. My son was suffering deeply and uncontrollably and I could do nothing to help him. No amount of reassuring, promising or begging could stop his tears or lessen his fears. My heart broke over and over again, night after night. It is every parent's worst nightmare to see their child suffering so horribly and not be

13

able to help them. I lived this nightmare every night for six months. Everyone I tried to ask advice from couldn't understand. They all gave extremely simple advice... Let him cry it out, make him stay in his own room, spank him. I had tried all but the spanking. I had been forceful, I had taken away favorite toys, and I had yelled and screamed. This only made matters worse. He would get more upset and uncontrollable at the time, and later he would cry and beg forgiveness and say he was sorry for being bad. It took awhile, but I finally gave up on trying to force my child to be better and decided instead to find a way to help him. No one will never know how guilty I now feel about those days and how much I regret them.

Finally, in desperation, I called our insurance company and asked for help. Thus began our five-year journey into the hell of mental health care. First of all, let me state that as a naïve person I assumed that these people had gone to school for this and that; they would know what they were doing. I eventually learned how wrong I could be. I have learned that just as in all professions, some people are great at what they do, while others are not. I have some very strong advice for anyone seeking mental health care. Ask for references, ask for specialties, research your options and do not be afraid to seek a second or even tenth opinion. These people are not God and from experience, I have learned that it usually takes three or four tries until a family finds a professional that actually helps them. For us, we are on our 10th. Do not be afraid to push for help if you are not happy and do not give up. You will have many fights ahead of you to secure the proper treatment for your child, so you will get lots of practice at being assertive. And always remember that you know your child best, so be sure to trust your instincts.

The Internet is an invaluable tool for doing research and finding information. There are a few support groups out there and they are composed of real parents who can give you recommendations on doctors and programs and insight from their own experiences. My favorite site is www.bpkids.org. They have a great message board that I spend hours reading and they have numerous links to helpful resources.

Back to our mental health care hell. The insurance coordinator set us up with a social worker. We drove to the next state over to see her because she was highly recommended. After an hour with her, it was clear that she was in over her head. She was used to helping children with the usual childhood fears. She had no idea what to do with Xanthe. She told me we needed to see a psychologist. I called the insurance coordinator with this request. I made an appointment with another "good" one.

This visit went a little better. This doctor seemed to understand our problems a little better. "Unfortunately," she said, "I can not completely help you. I will continue to do his therapy, but you need to take him to see a psychiatrist so that he can be prescribed some medications."

Of course, another professional. Why didn't I think of that? I didn't know at the time how the break down of titles worked and I was desperate for some immediate help. I wasn't sure how much longer Xanthe and I could go on like this. I wanted to scream when the psychologist told me that we needed to make yet another appointment. Each appointment so far had involved at least a three week wait. I wasn't sure we had that kind of time. Of course I called the insurance coordinator anyway. She was a little testy this time. It bothered me and I felt bad. Had I known then what I know now, I would have laughed. She was going to get even testier with time.

By the time our visit with the psychiatrist rolled around, we had driven from place to place, talked to numerous people, made millions of excuses to family and friends about his "weird" behavior and weeks had gone by. Xanthe was getting worse instead of better. This doctor did a quick evaluation and decided Xanthe had ADHD. She sent us home with a prescription for Adderall and instructions on seeking therapy to help with the symptoms. We left feeling pretty good. Finally a name for our hell and a medication to make it all go away. AGAIN, how wrong could I be!

Xanthe had always had strong cravings for carbohydrates and he was a little chubby. This ADHD medication was taking the pounds off quickly and he seemed to be concentrating better in school when we could get him there. For a very short time we were optimistic that we had found our answer. All of this was short lived though. He soon became extremely anxious. Worse than before. He needed even less sleep. Sometimes he could go a couple days without sleeping. He started lighting things on fire in the middle of the night and then he started picking at his skin until it bled when he was nervous. He said he couldn't sleep or concentrate because *things were running through his head very fast*. Sometimes these were scary things. If he tried to stop them or think of something else it just got worse.

One night I heard a scream coming from his bedroom. I almost killed myself running in there. In my panic I got tangled in the blankets, fell out of bed, ran into the door jam and smacked my arm against the wall all before I finally reached his room. During these long seconds he continued to scream. As I ran in I turned on the light. Since my eyes had not yet adjusted to the brightness of the room, the scene I saw was a little surreal. Xanthe's white comforter, that his nana had made him, looked to be covered in blood. I ran to him and scooped him up, blindly thinking I needed to rush him to the hospital. I tripped while carrying him and we both went down. He was still crying and I was searching his body for the fatal wound. Somehow I managed to see the situation for what it really was. Xanthe wasn't seriously wounded he had just picked the skin off of his arms and legs in huge patches. Once I calmed him down and I was able to breathe again, my first thought was that we had to go back to the doctor.

As luck would have it, that doctor was retiring. We were referred to a new psychiatrist. She took another history. This time we heard the words "bipolar disorder" for the first time. She kept the Adderall, but added an anti-psychotic medication called Seroquel. We left, filled the prescription and hit the bookstore for some information on this disorder. That is when I came across a very informative book called the *The Bipolar Child*. I highly recommend this book. I saw a lot of my son as I devoured the pages. The book contains some great real life scenarios, a checklist of symptoms of bipolar disorder, a great chapter on medications and tons of other helpful material. I spent the entire evening with the book. As I filled out the symptom checklist, I was shocked at how many things I had to mark. A lot of my questions had been answered, but now I had some new ones. I realized that my learning had just begun.

Fast-forward a few months. Some of Xanthe's symptoms were gone, but some new ones had appeared. He had stopped picking at his skin, but he was no longer the happy child I once knew. He was sad, depressed, irritable and anxious a lot. We continued seeing the same doctor, but nothing seemed to be helping. She had added an anti-depressant to his medication mix. Zoloft. I saw some changes after 3 months, but no real improvement in most of his behaviors. She was not very talkative and didn't really give us any advice. We stuck with her for two years though. I was still new to the mental health care world and I assumed that this must be as good as it was going to get or the doctor would have been more concerned.

For reasons I will never understand, Xanthe's symptoms were still present, but not as bad from 3rd grade to 6th grade. He still had nightmares, he wasn't sleeping all night, he was still extremely clingy and he had the irritability, depression and anxiousness. Even with these symptoms though, he still went to school more days than not and he wasn't as depressed when he was down or as active when he was manic as he had been. Even though our life was far from "normal," it was bearable and slightly improved, so we lived with it.

For these three years our lives looked somewhat normal to the outside world, but inside our house it was crazy. Everyday was a struggle; every night was a war. It was during this time that I developed my bad habits. I started giving into Xanthe on everything, hoping that his mood wouldn't sour. I walked on egg shells around him. His moods dictated my life. I went to sleep when he could, I left the house if he could handle it, I made and ate what he was willing to eat, I lived when and how his moods would let me live. It probably would have gone on like this forever if I hadn't met Chris (my present day fiancé). Since I had done such a great job of hiding Xanthe's illness from the outside world, all Chris saw was my complete submission to Xanthe.

One night Chris asked me about it and I broke down and cried.

For the first time, I was seeing our lives through different eyes. I realized that it must look like I was the crazy one, bowing to my son's every need and whim. This realization made me wish for the first time that people could see him sick. As bad as it sounds, life might have been easier for all of us if Xanthe looked sick or even if he had a socially acceptable illness that I could feel free to talk about. I had learned over the years that if I mentioned any of Xanthe's problems, people started to look at me differently and started to relate differently to Xanthe. I didn't want him to be labeled as "weird." People in general view mental illness as a character flaw, not a medical condition and I wasn't ready to subject my son to that.

Over the years I have come to believe that this public view of mental illness is caused as much by a lack of knowledge, as it is by a gross misunderstanding of the facts. Unfortunately, most movies, TV shows and books choose to portray mental illness in a bad light. The characters are almost always "crazy" people that can not be controlled or who go on to murder or harm their neighbors. Just as many people experience the loss of an elderly parent, yet no two react the same way, numerous people live with mental illness and no two react the same way. What the world needs is not an absolute understanding of mental illness (as this can never be attained, as you can never truly experience what another human being is experiencing), but a willingness to learn about the illnesses and the open-mindedness to support those that are striving to get better. I am not asking that all mentally ill people be babied and protected, I am asking for understanding and sympathy while the mentally ill are actively seeking a diagnosis and help. Even I have no patience for those that use their illness as a crutch and never try to help themselves. But I do feel for those that are trying and yet, are met with disapproval, prejudice and shame. Medicine, science and research have come along way and for most people there is help out there for their symptoms, if they choose to seek it.

I have three quotes that I often repeat to Xanthe in hopes that he will understand that he is the most important key to his future wellness and happiness. *As one goes through life one learns that if you don't paddle your own canoe, you don't move* (Katharine Hepburn), *God gives every bird his worm, but He does not throw it into the nest* (Swedish Proverb) and *It was on my fifth birthday that Papa put his hand on my shoulder and said, "Remember, my son, if you ever need a helping hand, you'll find one at the end of your arm"* (Sam Levenson).

What Chris said to me that night made me realize that I needed to let the people close to me see what was going on if I wanted their support and help in finding treatment for Xanthe. They needed to see and learn about the illness in order to help us. It was a very hard step. Everyone was shocked to find out what was going on. I had done such a great job of hiding our problems, that they had just assumed that over the years Xanthe had grown out of his little oddities and that all was well. Later, I had proof that it was a wise decision to tell everyone. Not long after I let our little secret out, our lives changed for the worse. I would not have been able to hide the truth if I had tried.

The middle of 6th grade turned out to be a turning point for us. Xanthe slipped into what I would now call a depression. He quit hanging out with his friends. He quit boy scouts and chess club. He stopped hanging out with family. He spent more and more time listening to music and banging on his drums. He was very angry about everything and so irritable, that we found it easier to not talk to him if we could avoid it. For weeks I chalked it up to adolescence. But as time went by, it became quite clear that something was seriously wrong. I tried discussing these changes with his psychiatrist, but she just increased his Zoloft. At one point during a session I asked her a question about Xanthe's behaviors and she studied her notes for a few minutes, looked at her watch and then announced the end of the session. I stared at her in disbelief. I repeated my question as she stood to usher us out the door. She murmured something about discussing it at the next session as she led us into the hall. Since she wasn't helping and I didn't want to waste anymore time, I decided to switch doctors, yet again. I put in another call to the insurance coordinator. Two days later we had an appointment with a new doctor.

This doctor seemed all right at first. I inform him of the bipolar diagnosis. I ask him if he agreed. He never directly answered me. He said that the Seroquel was helping with the mania, but we weren't really treating the depression. He put Xanthe on a high dose of Effexor and stopped the Zoloft. After four months on this regime Xanthe was worse than ever before. He was still very angry and irritable, but more anxious, moody and clingy than before. Then suddenly Xanthe was flat out incapable of going to school. He had severe anxiety attacks during class. He couldn't catch his breath, his whole body shook, and he would throw up on the floor and cry for me. Not a good thing to have happen in a classroom full of friends and peers. If he did stay at school he spent the entire time in the nurse's office crying. Sometimes he would eventually fall asleep in there. The school called me everyday, sometimes more than once. I spent more time on the phone with them or Xanthe than I did doing my work. I left early more days than not. If I did stay at work I was so stressed out and exhausted that I couldn't concentrate on the job at hand. I should have taken a leave of absence under FMLA, but the idea never occurred to me and no one ever mentioned it so instead I added the worry of losing my job to my already long list of concerns.

Our nights were even worse than our days during this time. Xanthe was scared most nights and others were filled with tears and statements of doom and hopelessness. After one particularly rough night I called the doctor. He got us an appointment two days later. The entire hour he acted distant. He just kept repeating that Xanthe was a very angry boy. At the end of the session I asked Xanthe to leave for a minute. I asked the doctor what I should do. He told me that all of Xanthe's problems stemmed from me. I was a bad mother. He said Xanthe was just an angry, spoiled boy. He also said something about seeing this a lot with rich parents who try to buy their children's love instead of spending time with them. I cried. I felt horrible. I called my mom. When I told her what the doctor had said, she immediately pointed out that I spend more time with my kids in one day than some moms do in a week. She also laughed about the rich parent part. Some months I had trouble paying the phone bill or even buying groceries. Having too much money had never been a concern of mine! Then she reminded me of all the facts I already knew about this disorder, all of the naïve opinions out there and, most importantly, of the fact that I do not have a sick daughter. If I was such a bad mom, wouldn't she be suffering in this way too?

I took my new found strength and called the insurance coordinator. She made a snide remark about my switching so often. I held my ground. She gave me a new name and number. By now I had learned a lot about researching mental health care. I went on the Internet to request some feedback on this new doctor and just for my own piece of mind, on the previous doctor. Lots of negative comments came back about the previous doctor. After reading about other's experiences with him, I decided to call and complain. Although nothing came of my complaint, it made me feel a little better.

Unfortunately, I did not receive any feedback about the new doctor before our first appointment. At first we liked this doctor. Within minutes of meeting us, she stated that Xanthe was definitely bipolar. She claimed he was on the wrong medications and she ordered a full medical work-up on him. That was something that had never been done before. We left feeling very hopeful.

At our second visit we had all the results back from the blood tests, ECG and so on. Other than the bipolar, he seemed very healthy. He was quite a bit overweight though, and that concerned her. Anti-psychotic medications are known to cause weight gain. Now for the funny part. She looked slowly from me to Xanthe to Tahni to their dad and back to me again and said, "You are all overweight, so I am going to write you a prescription for Jenny Craig or Weight Watchers."

First of all, she was right. We were all fat. With all the stress and ups and downs of our lives, I had taken to serving way too much fast food and prepackaged food. But what made this so funny, was that the doctor handing me this prescription was at least three times bigger than I was. It was a little hard to take the prescription without laughing.

We stuck with this doctor for a month or two until it became quite clear that she had one way, and one way only of dealing with bipolar children. When I asked around about my impression of her, many parents agreed and likened her to a dictator. The opinions about her methods were a toss up. She was great with some kids and horrible with others. While I am convinced that her way works with some kids, it was not working for my son and again, Xanthe was just getting worse. He had not been to school regularly for months. I was also beginning to feel discouraged. The doctor had taken to calling the school while Xanthe was there and speaking to the nurse about his day. The two of them would then make decisions regarding his treatment. Some days I would go in to pick Xanthe up (at noon or even 10am!) and the nurse would inform me of the new things I was to try. I was annoyed that I wasn't involved in these decisions. That's not to say I wouldn't have gone along with them for Xanthe's sake if they were working, but they weren't. Xanthe was getting more anxious and out of control by the day and he rarely stayed at school past 9am if he made it at all.

I called the happy insurance coordinator again. She was just thrilled to hear from me! After about thirty minutes of listening to her lecture me about sticking with one doctor and building a relationship with them, I finally got the name of a new doctor.

Our new doctor seemed nice and from what I read about her on the Internet, she was very experienced with bipolar children. She immediately pulled the Effexor and put him on a mood stabilizer. This was a first for us. After she explained what the purpose of the mood stabilizer was, I was very surprised that no other doctor had tried this approach before. Mood stabilizers are usually the first lines of medications prescribed for bipolar children. I was also a little angry. If a mood stabilizer is the first line of defense against these symptoms then why had the other doctors let him continue to suffer without it? His medications now consisted of Seroquel, Lamictal (mood stabilizer), Klonopin (anxiety) and of course, the Adderall. Xanthe's dad was again nervous about the addition of yet another medication. He worried about the long-term effects of prescribing and then taking away all of these medications. I, too, was a little worried, but I worked in pharmaceutical research and my medical background soothed most of my worries. From years of experience, we knew that all medications took time to work, so we headed home to wait. Little did we know what a horrible wait it would be.

I was scanning the message board of the bipolar web site when I saw the suggestion to journal my thoughts. It was supposed to help me sort out all of my feelings and I could also take it to our psychiatrist appointments so that the doctor could use the information written there to make decisions regarding Xanthe's treatment. Some people "chart" their children's behaviors and symptoms, but I liked the idea of writing my down in a journal like I was venting to an old friend. This way it would not only track all of the details of Xanthe's moods and symptoms, but I would get some therapeutic help by writing my feelings down as well. I decided to give it a try. At this point I would have tried anything and this idea seemed relatively easy! What follows is the story of our lives unfolding through the notes I made in my journal.

THURSDAY MARCH 14TH *(My first journal entry.)*

~ Xanthe is still not going to school. Every morning it is the same thing. Screams of terror, flowing tears and chopped up words as he gulps for air while begging to stay home. This morning he had me crying. It was hard to console him and I felt like I was losing my mind. A part of me just wanted to take him and Tahni into my room, close the door and shut out the world forever. The other part of me was mad. I was losing my patience. I dreaded hearing the superior tones of the school secretary when I called him in sick yet again. And I was selfishly upset at him. If he stayed home from school today then his hell would end for the moment, but mine would begin. I was going to be the one to take all the anger and snide remarks from the school, the kid's dad, Chris and everyone else, who thought I had given in. In the end, I called the school anyway. I got the feeling that they had given up on us and thought I was never going to be able to bring him back in, when they suggested that I apply for homebound services. I had never heard of this, but I told them that I would look into it.

Once I got to work I logged on to the bipolar web site. After learning a great deal about homebound services, I collapsed in relief. Finally, a way to end the morning struggles and keep Xanthe up on his school work. I felt a little like we had failed if we chose this option, but I also knew that we couldn't have gone on like this much longer. I immediately put in a call to the psychiatrist. I asked for a letter requesting homebound status and within hours she faxed two copies and a letter describing his current diagnosis.

After work I took it to the school. They informed me that it would be at least Monday before the services would go into effect. This meant that a tutor from the school district would come to our house every day for about an hour to teach Xanthe what his class was learning at school. I have to work during the day, so I was going to see if this could be done at his dad's house.

The school staff, of course, seemed ok with this arrangement, as they had been the ones to suggest it. Xanthe's dad was willing to give it a try and Chris was annoyed. He thinks it is ridiculous that Xanthe can't go to school. He doesn't want us to talk about it. Xanthe seemed ok with the idea, but of course, he was anxious! Tahni asked what she was supposed to tell all the kids at school when they ask where Xanthe was. I had no answers for her and I felt terrible. She has had to grow up so quickly. Everyday she has to face things that most adults can not even deal with. She is a strong kid. I hope I am doing right by her.

MONDAY MARCH 18TH

~ We had a terrible weekend. I should have written it all down as it happened, but I am still getting used to this journal. Xanthe had three really bad nights. Nightmares and depression for one night, then mania and no need for sleep for two nights. Of course, I was up with him all three times.

When he has nightmares, they are about things like my death or him being kidnaped and they are real. There is no way to calm him down. I just hold him, let him cry and do my best to reassure him.

The depression is just as bad. He points out all of the things that are wrong with his life and I never have any answers. No matter what I say he has a counter point to prove that life is worthless. It makes me cry to see him this sad and hopeless.

The mania is tough too. He is hyper, needs no sleep and has a thousand projects going on at once. He, of course, wants all the supplies for these projects right now and he gets very upset if I tell him no. They are crazy projects like cures for cancer and lotions that cure backaches. When I drifted off to sleep for a few a minutes Saturday night, I awoke to find that he had mixed some strange concoction up and he wanted to rub it on my back. It looked bad and smelled worse. There was an urgency in his eyes though, so I agreed to try the lotion. Right or wrong, I claimed it worked in hopes that he would settle down for the night. Instead he went off on a rampage about how to patent and market the stuff. He got very angry when I

25

refused to call the department of patents at two o'clock in the morning. HELP!

The school called today. They will be starting the tutoring on Wednesday. We set it up to take place at his dad's house. The school is confident that this will work and that Xanthe will stay current enough to pass the 6th grade. I have my doubts though. He is way behind right now. I have to wonder if the school really believes that he can stay current on his school work or if they are just tired of dealing with us. Chris thinks it's the latter.

We had a psychiatrist appointment today. I expressed my concern that the medications were still not working. She talked to Xanthe for awhile and then decided to increase his dosage of Lamictal, while lowering his dose of Seroquel. She wants him off of the Seroquel by the end of the week. I was too tired and confused to question her. I just crossed my fingers and hoped that she was right.

WEDNESDAY MARCH 20TH

~ This morning I dropped Tahni off at school, then dropped Xanthe off at his dad's and headed to work. Xanthe was very groggy from his medications, and the fact that he had not been sleeping well at all. I crossed my fingers and hoped the day would go well.

I sat at work staring at my computer. I could not concentrate. All of these questions keep running through my mind. Will the tutor be able to teach Xanthe? Will he learn enough to pass 6th grade? How is all of this affecting Tahni? Am I missing something? Maybe there is something more I should be doing? Some stone unturned that would be the key to the answer for all of this? I got up and walked out to my car. I just needed a minute in the sun to get my head together. For the millionth time I wished there was a training class for this that taught you all (or even a few!) of the answers.

Later, I found out that the tutoring session had gone well. It was more of a "get to know you" kind of session. She did leave a bunch of work that Xanthe needed to make up. We tried to do homework after dinner, but Xanthe was a mess. Up then down ,then up again.

Very irritable and easily frustrated. I made a bad decision and decided to cheat. Even worse I involved my mom in it. I decided to do some of Xanthe's makeup work on the computer just to help him get caught up. He was so far behind and I knew he would never get it all done in the state he was in. In my stressed out, frustrated, exhausted state it actually seemed like a good idea. My mom and I laughed at the situation as we typed out the work. It felt like some crazy episode of the "Twighlight Zone." Mom said we laughed so we wouldn't cry. She is awesome. Without her I would have given up by now. I ask way too much of her, but she never complains and she is always there for me. I owe her more than I can ever repay.

I sat Xanthe down to complete what was left of his make-up work around eight o'clock. It started out ok, but then he got very frustrated. That led to crying and then to hopelessness.

"I will never learn this stuff, I am dumb, something is wrong with me, why is this so hard? Why can't I just be like the other kids?" he screamed out between sobs.

I tried to help. I told him he was smart. That just made things worse.

He screamed, "You don't understand!" and ran out of the room. *No, I don't understand*, I thought, but I wished I did. I wished I could just take this all away. It is so hard to watch him struggle so much. I followed him into the other room. He was lying on the floor, curled up into a ball, crying. I tried to console him, but he just kept crying and talking about how horrible life was. I sat on the floor next to him for awhile, rubbing his back then eventually when I felt as though I could do no more to help him, I got up and joined the rest of the family to watch TV. I felt like a failure. About thirty minutes later I went back in to check on him. He had fallen asleep on the floor. It pained my heart to look at him lying there. He looked so sad and alone. I felt horrible for leaving him to deal with his pain by himself. How was a twelve year old supposed to deal with this? I woke him up just enough to lead him onto the sofa so I could hold him. He whimpered and frowned as he slept fitfully beside me. It hurt me to see him so unhappy even in sleep. No more homework for tonight!

FRIDAY MARCH 22ND

~ The tutoring on Thursday went about the same, and the tutor didn't come today. She is only required to teach him for five hours a week, so instead of an hour a day, she wants to break it up into three sessions a week. She is going to work the schedule out with Xanthe's dad.

We tried to have a normal, fun evening tonight. I rented a movie that Xanthe had chosen and we ordered some pizza. Before the movie we played a board game. The game went pretty well, but at one point Xanthe got mad at his sister for the way she played her turn. It wasn't that big of a deal, but Xanthe can get out of control sometimes. He started screaming at her, saying that he was going to kill her and his hands were clenched at his sides. I saw the telltale redness in his face and the look in his eyes. I knew he was about to loose control. I stood up and dragged him into the other room. Even though these situations always play out the same way, I was still hurt by what he said and at a loss as to how to make it turn out differently. He accused me of always taking her side, of never understanding. He claimed that his life was horrible and unfair. He slammed his fist into the breakfast bar. He said he hated his life and all of us. I just stood there taking it all and trying to reassure him that I still loved him. Eventually, like it always does, his anger fizzled out and he began to cry. He went on to apologize for being so bad and for ruining our evening. I could see the fear and shame in his eyes. He told me he loved me over and over again. He begged me not to be mad at him. I consoled him as best I could and then made him go in and apologize to his sister. At first Tahni was still mad, but eventually she forgave him. That is usually how it goes. She has forgiven him more times than anyone can count. I am not sure why or even how she does it. He says some pretty hurtful things to her when he is like this. She seems to have an understanding of his illness way beyond her years and has the patience of a saint.

MONDAY MARCH 25TH

~ Xanthe had me up late again last night. This time he was again going on and on about how pathetic his life was. He kept talking about what a horrible skate boarder he was and how he would never get any better. I tried to tell him all the usual parent stuff. Practice makes perfect. No one is good when they first learn a new skill. He dismissed everything I said. His train of thought eventually lead to him talking about how horrible he was at everything in life and what a loser he was, how he couldn't even go to school like normal kids. I tried to be positive, but everything I said, he shot down with words of gloom. It was a long night, and I am sure that I did not handle it very well.

I did go into work this morning, but I didn't take Xanthe to his dad's. The tutor wasn't coming today, and Xanthe seemed to be ok with staying by himself. He slept most of the day, while I tried to keep my eyes open and concentrate.

Our evening was uneasy. Xanthe was agitated all night. His irritability and restlessness put us all on guard. It was as if we were waiting for hell to break loose. I tried all through dinner and the early evening to change Xanthe's mood, but nothing worked. As I washed the dinner dishes, I tried to mentally prepare myself for what I was sure was going to be a long night. Xanthe surprised me though around 9pm when he announced that he was going to bed. He seemed frustrated with us and his own mood and he just wanted to be left alone. Before I headed to bed about an hour later, I looked in on him. He was listening to music and tapping his drumsticks in the air to the beat. I thought about interrupting him and trying to talk, but after several minutes of staring I decided to leave well enough alone and head to bed. I figured that if he needed me later, he knew where to find me! I stayed up for another hour expecting to hear him at my door, but he never came. I finally turned out the lights and crawled under the covers, but I couldn't relax. With every creak in the house I turned my head expecting to see my door open, and when it never did I eventually gave in and went to sleep.

WEDNESDAY APRIL 3RD

~ Life is staying the same, no matter what we try or do. If anything, life is getting worse. As Xanthe's illness progresses, more and more of life's normal routines are becoming too much for him. Now he is having problems with staying home by himself. He fears that someone will break in. I find this fear of his very hard to understand. Not only have we never had a break in, but we do not know anyone who has. If we had I would chalk it up to post-traumatic stress, but since we haven't, I am at a loss as to where the fear comes from.

We keep trying different dosage amounts and different therapy ideas, but Xanthe is still very moody and anxious. He is still not sleeping at night, and his moods are more depressed than happy nowadays. The tutor has also had quite a time with him. He is either half-asleep for the entire session or extremely grumpy. I think she might be losing her patience with him. He is keeping up with the homework though, and no, my mother and I are not doing it!

Our evening went fairly well today. Xanthe was clingy as usual, and we cuddled a lot while we watched TV. For most of the evening he was quiet. When he did talk, it was to seek reassurances for his fears. I stayed up with him after everyone else had gone to bed. We talked quietly until he fell asleep in my arms. I waited fifteen minutes to make sure he was out, then I headed to bed.

SATURDAY APRIL 6TH

~ Today started out normal enough. We all slept in because Xanthe had us up late last night. I made us all breakfast, and then we lounged around until it was time to take the kids to their dad's. I have to admit that I was really looking forward to a night without them. I was tired and stressed out. Plus, my shoulder was hurting. I assumed it was because I had slept on it wrong.

After the kids were gone, my mom and I sat around watching

"girly" shows and tried to relax. Chris had gone over to his parent's house for dinner. Every time the phone rang, I jumped in panic that it was something bad about Xanthe.

As the evening wore on, the pain in my shoulder started to increase. I took some aspirin, but the pain just got worse. Before long my entire left arm hurt and I was finding it hard to breathe. Every time I took a breath, a pain shot through my chest. At first I wasn't going to mention it to my mom, but as the pain worsened I started to get scared. Finally I told her, and she immediately wanted to take me to the hospital. I tried to refuse. She said that if I called the ask-a-nurse hotline and they said I didn't have to go, then she wouldn't make me. I called them partly because she made me and partly because I was very scared. After thirty minutes on the phone with the nurse, it was decided that I needed to go to the emergency room. I tried to play the whole thing off, like it bothered me that a little pain was going to ruin our girl's night. Chris was still at his parent's and wouldn't be home for hours so I didn't bother to call him. More of my attempt to be casual about the entire ordeal.

Once at the hospital though I really started to take my symptoms seriously. When the nurse did the intake evaluation my blood pressure was 180 over 112. Seeing as the normal reading is 120 over 80, I was in trouble. I knew from my medical background that this could lead to a stroke if it got any higher.

As I sat back down next to my mom in the waiting room, I could tell that she sensed something, but I chose not to tell her anything about it. I was still trying to deny that anything was wrong. I figured that if I didn't say it out loud, it wouldn't be real. I was too scared to face reality. *Who would take care of my babies if I couldn't? How would Xanthe ever survive if I died?* That last thought brought tears to my eyes. I quickly made a promise to God that I would only do good things with my life, if he promised to let me live until Xanthe was 20 years old. I figured by that time Xanthe could survive the loss of me.

The nurse eventually took me back to a room and drew a ton of blood samples and did an ECG. While we were waiting for the results, I told my mom about the high reading. I could tell she was scared. She looked as though she might cry. She offered to go call Chris, but I convinced her to wait until we had the results. We made strained small talk as we waited to find out my fate.

Eventually, the doctor came in and told me the good news. I was just too stressed out. My body was warning me that if I didn't start sleeping better and reducing my stress level, I could be headed for trouble. I was relieved, but also scared. How in the world was I supposed to relieve this stress or even sleep better?

Mom and I laughed on the way home. We made little jokes about a wasted evening and missing our favorite shows. We were both trying to cover our feelings of fear and relief. I finally called Chris while mom drove and told him what had happened. He was mad that I had never told him I was going , but relieved that I was all right. I made up a different reason for the pain though. I knew he would be mad if he thought that Xanthe had caused it. He was always mad if something went wrong because of our problems with Xanthe. We argue about it all the time. It was just easier to lie (again).

MONDAY APRIL 8TH

~ I called in sick to work today. I was still hurting a little and I figured that since the kids were still at their dad's, I could sleep in and try to relax. I was wrong. I spent the entire day worried about both Xanthe and Tahni. I couldn't wait until it was time to pick Tahni up from school and then go get Xanthe at his dad's. For some reason, I always feel better when they are around. Part of it is because I feel guilty for wanting time away from them, the other part is that I want to be there to console them if they need me.

I had told the kids' dad about my hospital trip, and that is why he had kept them an extra day. When I got them home, I told them a little about it, but again I lied about the cause. (Lying has become my best skill over the years.) They treated me like a queen all night because they thought I was sick. They brought me drinks and pillows and gave me hugs. Tahni even made me a get-well soon card.

Bedtime, unfortunately, was bad again. I do not know if it was because Xanthe had been at his dad's all weekend, or because I was sick, or if it would have happened anyway. Xanthe was anxious and scared all night. He said he had bad thoughts running through his head, and he couldn't stop them. We cuddled on the sofa and named 80's rock bands together. That sometimes gets his mind occupied and calms him down. He loves eighties hair bands!

TUESDAY APRIL 9TH

~ Tutoring went badly today. Xanthe was very groggy, and he kept falling asleep. The tutor expressed her unhappiness about it to Xanthe's dad. He tried to apologize and blamed it on the medications. Eventually she gave up and just left some work for Xanthe to do when he woke up. Xanthe's dad called me at work to explain about the tutor and suggested I try to find a way to keep Xanthe more alert. Yeah, OK, I will get right on that. I am so tired of having to explain to everyone that his sedation is part of the reason he is on homebound status. If we took the kind of powerful medications that he did, we would be wiped out too!

Xanthe was especially down when I got him home. He was sad and irritable. I tried a few times to cheer him up, but that just made it worse. He was upset about the tutor and upset that everyone wanted him to try harder. He stated over and over again that he was trying, but he was just too tired. For the rest of the evening I tried to reassure him that we understood, but my words were just that… words. I could tell that he didn't believe me. By bedtime we were both tired of fighting his bad mood so I gave him some Benadryl to make him fall asleep. I slept restlessly though. Every time I heard a noise, I sat up thinking it was Xanthe. A few times I went into check on him. He was sleeping restlessly also. He kept tossing and turning and yelling out "no" in his sleep.

THURSDAY APRIL 11ᵀᴴ

~ The tutoring session went badly again today. Xanthe was irritable and didn't want to pay attention. The tutor called the school expressing her concern. She was wondering why Xanthe couldn't go to school. She stated that he didn't seem sick and that he wasn't willing to learn. The school called me shortly after they heard from her to tell me what she had said. I called the district office to try and soothe things over. I asked them if they had ever worked with bipolar children before. They assured me that they had. I informed them anyway of the symptoms and side effects of this illness and explained why Xanthe couldn't function in school. I also stressed that Xanthe was more than willing to learn, that he was very upset that he couldn't ,and that if it were at all possible for him, he would be doing better. They assured me that they would speak to the tutor. I hung up feeling stressed out and frustrated. I didn't really believe that they had understood me. And I was scared. *What would I do if the tutor quit? How would I keep Xanthe current enough to pass the sixth grade?*

After work, I ran through the drive-thru for dinner and then headed home. I was getting very tired of fast food, but I also knew that I might have a long night ahead of me and I didn't feel like adding clean-up to the list.

Bedtime went better than expected. I think Xanthe had worn himself out at his dad's worrying about the tutor. I was able to get him relaxed and asleep earlier than usual, and Chris was still awake when I finally came to bed. That gave us a few moments alone. We talked and tried to reconnect.

FRIDAY APRIL 12ᵀᴴ

~ The tutor called today and said she couldn't make it to the session. Something about a time conflict. I wondered for a second whether the excuse was real or if she was giving up on Xanthe. I hadn't had a chance to talk with her since I had called the district. I had already taken Xanthe to his dad's, so he stayed there until I got home from work. His dad informed me that he had slept most of the day.

Xanthe was tired all evening so our night was pretty uneventful. He played video games, did some make-up work and watched TV. By 9pm he was pretty groggy. I sat up with him for a little while to make sure he was going to be OK, and then I finally went to bed.

While lying in bed last night ,Chris had brought up the idea of moving again. We had talked about moving to the "country" off and on for about three years now. Chris sounded pretty serious this time, though. I knew all the pros and cons of moving by heart.

Pros: Xanthe would have room to ride his 4-wheeler, and we would have a pond so that he could fish. With a lot of land, we would all have room to get away from each other if tensions ran high. We could get a pool. We could start over in a new neighborhood and school where everyone didn't think we were crazy. Chris could have a garage.

Cons: The kids would have to switch schools. Not a real problem for Xanthe since he would be going to a new school for junior high next year anyway, but a big deal to Tahni. She was dead set against switching and leaving her friends. We would be far away from my mom, whom I had began to feel I couldn't live without, and the kids' dad, who took them on the weekends and helped out whenever he could during the week. The drive to work would be a killer. The monthly payment would go up tremendously, and I called in sick to work a lot because of this illness. I worried that we wouldn't be able to afford it. We wouldn't live so close to other people, and the kids might not have anyone to play with. And it was change, something that scared me right now.

Since Chris was so set on moving though, I agreed to look around. I really didn't think we would find anything very soon, so I figured I had some time to come up with a plan to hold off on the move. Or at least to come to terms with moving and make some adjustments in our lives to make it run more smoothly.

SUNDAY APRIL 14TH

~ While flipping through the Sunday paper, Chris realized how pricey land could be. This put him in a bad mood for the rest of the day. Xanthe was mad too. He had wanted to go riding today, but after Chris was finished looking at the paper he was in too foul a mood to take him. They both sulked around the house for hours. I tried a few times to cheer each of them up, but they just brushed me off and stayed angry.

I tried to get some house cleaning done, but Tahni followed me around complaining of being bored. She went on and on about how we never get to do anything together. She always says that I am busy with Xanthe, tired or cleaning. She informed me, in a not so happy tone, that she was sick of it and stomped off to her room. Before I had time to react to her, Xanthe hit me with his version of how much today sucked. I stood in the kitchen and cried.

Dinner was fun. Everyone ate in silence. Every once in a while someone would speak up long enough to complain and then we would be back to silence again. I tried to get the conversation going a few times, but I was too tired to give it any real effort. I finally settled for enjoying my dinner in peace.

Bedtime was easier than I thought it would be. Chris and Tahni turned in early because they were both still mad. Xanthe was upset also, but he wanted to play video games. I dosed him with Benadryl, watched him play and listened to him complain. About an hour later his eyelids were closing and the controller fell out of his hands. I tucked him in on the sofa and went to bed.

MONDAY APRIL 15TH

~ I am tired today. Life doesn't seem to be getting any better. Xanthe is still suffering and the change in medications doesn't seem to have done much good. We had another appointment with the psychiatrist today. It went about the same. More concern from

Xanthe's dad and me, more medication changes from the doctor. I asked for the millionth time if she thought we were getting any closer to stability. She answered the same as she always does, "These things take time and trial and error."

Was that supposed to make me feel better? I wondered, because it just made me feel worse. I have been trying to be patient for awhile now, but there is only so much a person can take.

Xanthe was very depressed tonight. He said he was tired of all the medication and tired of trying. He was mad that nothing was working. He was even more upset that life was getting worse. With all the therapy that we went through and all the medications that he swallowed, he was expecting to be getting better, but instead he was not going to school, he had lost most of his friends, and his self-esteem was close to non-existent, due to all the people he felt he had let down by not improving.

From his spot on the sofa, wrapped in my arms, he looked up at me with sad eyes and said, "You said that this would get better, that going to these doctors would help me. I don't believe in doctors anymore."

I didn't even try to hide my tears this time. I just held him and we both cried.

WEDNESDAY APRIL 17TH

~ Today I came to the realization that I am addicted to cola. Pop, soda, whatever you want to call it, has a huge hold on me. Last night around 8pm I went to the refrigerator to grab a can and realized we were out. I stood there contemplating a trip to the store. Finally, I decided I didn't want to get out so I grabbed a glass of milk instead. Unfortunately, I realized too late that I should have gone to the store. All night long I dreamt of cola. Drinking it, tasting it, even once I was swimming in it. I woke up at 5 a.m. this morning needing a cola so badly that I went to the store in my pajama pants to buy some. I didn't even wait until I got home to drink it. I just popped open a can right there in the store. I am sure I was quite a sight. Unbrushed hair, still sleepy eyes and a desperation on my face for cola. It's a good thing they didn't try to have me committed.

Once home, I thought about my addiction. I realized that it had become a habit of sorts. I no longer ate breakfast or lunch. I just grabbed a can of cola out of the refrigerator. It was easy and it tasted good. I tried to count how many cans I thought I drank in a day. I only know for sure that it has to be at least 10. Maybe more. *Do they have a support group for this?* I wondered as I put the newly bought cans away.

Tutoring went badly again today. The tutor left after only 20 minutes ,saying that she couldn't teach Xanthe if he wouldn't work with her. She did leave a bunch of homework though. Great, I thought when I found out, another night of fighting to get it all done.

Our evening was hell. Xanthe struggled through every aspect of his make-up work. The entire family argued through dinner. TV viewing was just as bad. Everyone argued over who should sit where and what we would watch. By 9pm I was ready to collapse. I dosed Xanthe with Benadryl, tucked Tahni in for the night and then fell onto the sofa. By 11pm Xanthe's anger had fizzled out and he was fast asleep. I contemplated sleeping right where I was, but eventually forced myself to get up and go to bed. What a horrible day it had been.

SATURDAY APRIL 20TH

~ Tomorrow is Easter Sunday. Of course, we have an entire day planned of family festivities. I am dreading it like the plague. Family gatherings and Xanthe do not get along. There is always so much excitement and too many things going on at once. Before the day is over at least ten people will have asked Xanthe to talk softer and slow down. He always tries to be in every conversation. He makes things up if he doesn't know anything about the topic. He tries too hard to fit in, since most of his life he hasn't. His effort to be "just like everyone else" is a little over the top and it hurts me to see him try so hard, but it generally just annoys everyone else. After awhile he gets on people's nerves.

Or the day can go another way with Xanthe being sad and depressed. In that instance, he follows me around and complains about everything and eventually ends up crying and we have to go home.

On holidays, I spend the entire day trying to stay one step ahead. I try to steer conversations around Xanthe. I try to interrupt when I sense that he is getting long-winded. I try to redirect him to other activities when I can tell that a certain group has tired of him. I try to make sure Tahni is having fun. I try to make sure Chris isn't getting too annoyed at Xanthe, and if I sense that he is then I try to soothe Chris over before it gets out of hand. I think Chris gets embarrassed for him and doesn't know how to handle it so he usually just gets mad.

I am also busy avoiding everyone's prying questions. *Why can't Xanthe go to school? What did you say his problem was? He looks fine to me, are you sure he's really sick?* A part of me wants to sit them down and explain the entire ordeal, but another part of me is afraid. I have a hard enough time trying to get Chris to be supportive, let alone extended family. I am afraid that they will look down on Xanthe for the behavior they are witnessing, but I am equally afraid that they will look down on him more if they know the whole story. By the end of the day I am exhausted. I HATE FAMILY GATHERINGS!

MONDAY APRIL 22ND

~ Easter went just as I thought it would, but all in all we had a good time. Xanthe thought he was too old for an Easter egg hunt, but I made him do it anyway. It didn't hurt that the eggs were filled with dollar bills instead of candy.

The tutor came today. She was impressed with the work that Xanthe had done, but annoyed about the work he hadn't finished. She was also irritated that Xanthe was so tired. Xanthe's dad tried to explain that he'd had a big weekend, but the tutor didn't think that that should have mattered. She left early, clearly frustrated and annoyed.

Xanthe had a tough time falling asleep tonight. He was upset that the tutor was mad at him and upset that he felt so far behind. He has taken to feeling paranoid about not passing the sixth grade. No amount of reassurance seems to calm him down. I have to wonder if part of the problem is that I, too, am afraid that he will not pass the sixth grade. I know that children can sense things even if you try to hide them. I just can not completely shake the fear of failure.

By the time Xanthe fell asleep on the sofa, I realized I was too exhausted to sleep. I tried watching TV and then reading a book, but neither distraction could ease my mind. I finally settled for a night of lying in bed staring at the ceiling, sorting through a sea of what ifs.

THURSDAY APRIL 25TH

~ The tutor didn't come Tuesday or Wednesday. She claimed that she had prior commitments. I am still fearful that she is avoiding Xanthe or giving up on him. She did come today though, and she spent 3 hours with him. That has to be a good sign. I had spent all night last night stressing the importance of these sessions to Xanthe. I had him convinced that he had to try harder and be nicer so that she would finish out the year. I realized that everything I was saying he already knew, but I figured it didn't hurt to try. I guess a little of it must have sunk in (or he was just having a good day) because he was on his best behavior today. He even managed to make her laugh once.

Since his session with the tutor went well, he was in a better mood tonight. In fact, it was one of those rare nights where Xanthe and Tahni actually played together for a few hours without it resulting in a fight. Tahni was having a great time, and I could tell that she was disappointed when Xanthe finally lost interest and decided to watch TV. I didn't want her fun to end ,so I asked her to play cards with me. She jumped at the idea, and we had a great time. The fact that she beat me every time didn't hurt either!

To ensure that Xanthe had an easy time falling asleep, I gave him two Benadryl with his evening medications. Sometimes this works and sometimes it doesn't, but I was hoping for the best. I really needed to get some sleep!

Luckily for me the medication worked and Xanthe was asleep by 10pm. It took my last ounce of strength to walk to bed. I hit the pillow already half asleep.

SATURDAY APRIL 27TH

~ Last night was horrible. Xanthe and I were up until 3am this morning. He started out hyper at bedtime. He wanted to play video games, but he wanted me to watch him. If I tried to leave the room, even to go to the bathroom, he got upset. Around midnight I told him that I couldn't stay up any longer. He started to cry. At first I was mad. I felt like he was manipulating me. But then he started in with his explanation. He was scared. He said that he had seen a strange car drive by our house ten times today. He knew that they were waiting for us all to go to sleep so that they could come in and kill us. I wanted to yell at him, to shake some sense in to him, to get him to understand that nobody was waiting to kill us. Instead, I just listened. He described the car, the man driving it and explained what he thought the guy's plan was. I think it made him feel better to tell someone, because after we talked, he seemed to be a little more relaxed. That gave me an idea. I tried to explain to him that it wasn't his job to keep us safe. That the adults are the ones that will take care of the burglars. This didn't relax him as I thought it would. He just calmly explained to me that adults are always tired at night so he had to be the one to stay up and listen for a break in. I sighed with defeat. There really was no way to reach this kid.

I decided to stay up with him until the anxiety ran its course. We played video games, checked the locks, talked, checked the locks, cuddled and checked the locks. He eventually fell asleep next to me on the sofa. I didn't want to wake him so we both slept there.

Chris was mad when he woke up and realized I had never come to bed. He gets quiet when he is mad. All morning I tried to engage him in conversation, but he kept his answers curt.

At noon I took the kids to their dad's for the night. I was relieved that they were going. I needed a break from the worry, and I needed some alone time with Chris to try and work things out. On the drive home I contemplated not talking to Chris at all. The exhausted part of me just wanted to go home, drink a glass of wine and fall into, what I hoped would be, a dreamless sleep. The smarter part of me knew that I had to try to talk to Chris. With everything that went on every day, our relationship sometimes got lost in the shuffle. I was really slacking on my half of the deal.

Making up with Chris did not go as I had planned. We argued mostly, then gave each other the silent treatment. I ended up having that glass of wine and going to bed. We slept facing opposite sides of the room. Needless to say, I did not fall into a dreamless sleep.

SUNDAY APRIL 28TH

~ I slept late and then had to hurry to get the kids picked up on time. Chris surprised me when we returned home. He had both of the 4-wheelers loaded up and asked Xanthe if he wanted to go riding. I looked at him with questions in my eyes. He came over to me, kissed me and then whispered in my ear, "Sorry about last night. Maybe if we go riding you can relax and spend some time with Tahni."

I thanked him with a kiss of my own. Even though we argue a lot, Chris is a great guy. I respect him for what he is doing. I know how hard it is to remain patient and understanding with Xanthe, and he is my flesh and blood child. Chris does it every day also and Xanthe is his "stepson." It takes a great man to do what Chris does on a daily basis.

Tahni and I had a great day, even though she was a little annoyed when I took a quick nap. I made it up to her by taking her out for dinner, just the two of us. I let her pick the restaurant, and she quickly decided on one that Chris and Xanthe do not like. We had a great time talking and eating for over two hours. We were almost disappointed when we pulled in the driveway and realized the boys were home.

Bedtime was good though. Chris was in a better mood and Xanthe was tired from riding. Getting him to sleep only took an hour, and I was able to go to bed when Chris did. We spent a little time talking and cuddling, then gave in and turned out the lights. It was nice to fall asleep in his arms for a change.

TUESDAY APRIL 30TH

~ Xanthe called me repeatedly today at work to tell me that he was scared, even though he was at his dad's. I must have looked upset because my boss stopped by to ask me what was wrong. All the stress of the last few months just came to a head with that one question, and I started crying and pouring out my entire life story. After ushering me into her office for a little privacy, she eventually she sent me home for the rest of the day. Xanthe was subdued and tired when I got him home, but very happy to be with me. I think he wore himself out worrying about being away from me.

Xanthe took a nap while I made dinner. Chris and Tahni watched TV. I used the quiet in the kitchen to contemplate Xanthe's mood today. Most days he was OK at his dad's. I had to wonder if something had happened to set him off. This whole 'missing me thing' is very hard to predict. Sometimes he can stay at his dad's all weekend and not even call me at all. Other times I can not even go to the store without him. I think part of the problem might be that from early on, I was the only one around who tried to understand and comfort him. Now, even though others are trying very hard, Xanthe feels most comfortable with me. I guess I just need to be patient and understanding while we wait for his trust to deepen in other people.

By bedtime, Xanthe was wide awake and anxious. He spent the night begging me to stay home tomorrow and I spent it insisting that I had to go. We played this depressing game for hours until sleep overtook him and he relaxed in my arms.

WEDNESDAY MAY 1ST

~ Xanthe was still sleeping when I left for work, but by the time I arrived there he had called three times. I played the messages immediately. Each one sounded more desperate than the last. I called home and Tahni answered. She told me that Xanthe was scared and wanted me to come home. When Xanthe came on the line I explained to him that I left early yesterday so I couldn't leave today. He started to cry. I told him to hang in there and I would see what I could do.

I called everyone I knew to see if I could beg them to go sit with Xanthe. No luck. Finally, I went to see my boss and ask if I could take an early and extended lunch. When she agreed I literally ran to the car and raced home. Imagine my surprise when I walked in and Xanthe was happily playing video games with the neighbor's son! I looked to Tahni for an explanation and she just shrugged her shoulders like *Who ever knows?* I pulled Xanthe into the kitchen to explain. He quickly stated, "I am fine now. Can I please get back to my game?"

I wanted to strangle the kid. All that worry for nothing. Instead I grabbed a cold pop from the fridge, kissed Tahni goodbye and headed back to work. All in all, the entire ordeal took an hour and he didn't even need me. I just added the experience to my pile of crazy stories to tell the grandkids!

For the rest of the day at work I kept expecting the phone to ring, but it never did and Xanthe was still fine when I finally arrived home. His great mood even lasted through dinner and bedtime. At 9pm he wasn't tired so he decided to stay up and play video games while we all headed to bed. I walked to my room wondering how long he was going to make it on his own. I tried to fall asleep, but I was too wired, waiting for Xanthe to make an appearance beside my bed. I decided to count sheep, but it didn't work. Instead I decided to make an early mental Christmas list. I had tons of ideas for everyone, and it was easy to concentrate on. Finally, my eyelids became too heavy to hold open and I fell asleep. The last time I had checked the clock it was 1am.

FRIDAY MAY 3ʳᴰ

~ I actually got to stay at work all day today, and I didn't even have to take a lunch! Xanthe seemed fine all day until dinner. I was making chicken enchiladas and he wanted tacos. He followed me around the kitchen whining and begging for tacos. I finally had enough and yelled, "What is your problem? It is just dinner. If you don't like it, eat a bowl of cereal!"

Of course, that made him cry. Through his sobs, he explained that he had seen a show on TV about people getting sick from eating chicken and he didn't want me to die. I felt horrible for yelling at him. I asked a bunch of questions about the show and was finally able to convince him that our chicken was fine. He retreated to his room. By the time dinner was ready, he was totally over the entire thing, and he ate three helpings. I just can't seem to keep up!

His sudden happiness lasted all evening. He was hyper and full of ideas. He eventually roped his sister into trying some of them out with him. They played together in her room for hours. This time it was Tahni that called an end to their fun. She was tired and just wanted to sit by me on the sofa. We cuddled and talked about her day at school while Xanthe ran around the house building things and searching for supplies.

I gave Xanthe two Benadryl to help him sleep, but he was too wound up. I eventually went to bed and he stayed up for who knows how long by himself. I kept expecting him to come wake me, but he never did.

SUNDAY MAY 5TH

~ We all woke up fairly early this morning, and I made a real breakfast while Chris drove down to buy a paper. He was set on searching for some land. The kids and I ate, laughed and talked while Chris searched the real estate section. Eventually he looked up to tell us about a house on 5 acres that he found. Before he even read us the description, he announced that he wanted to go look at it. It's a three-bedroom house with a two-car garage and a pond. Lots of room for the dogs to roam, for Xanthe to ride, and for us to put in a pool. Everyone was very excited.

We spent the rest of the day talking off and on about actually owning a house like that. The possibilities we came up with were endless. I started laughing after one suggestion and pointed out that in order to fit in all the things we wanted, we had better start looking at one hundred acres ,not five. Tahni wants an in-ground heated pool, a trampoline and a dance studio. Xanthe wants an acre large pond, a four-wheeler track and some hunting ground. Chris wants a huge pole barn, a second unattached garage (for his toys!) and enough land to necessitate the need for a tractor. I just want a hot tub and enough room for our stuff. And maybe a sound proof room where I can scream to let off steam!

By bedtime we were all in great spirits. We had a wonderful dinner and we were still excited. Xanthe even went to sleep without any problems because his mind was busy planning his new room, his pond and his track.

MONDAY MAY 6TH

~ Chris called about the house while he was at work today. He had made an appointment to see it at five. I made him mad when I explained that I couldn't go. I had taken off a lot recently, and I was trying to make some of it up. He angrily decided to go by himself. I hung up feeling exhausted. *Why did everything have to be a fight? Couldn't he just understand and support me? Maybe change the appointment to tomorrow? Jeesh, why did he have to be so stubborn?*

The minute Chris walked through the door, I asked him about the house. He tersely explained that he had cancelled the appointment, then he stomped off toward our bedroom. I just shook my head. Now I had to deal with a third child!

Dinner went well enough, even though Chris was being quiet. Xanthe was still in a great mood and he and Tahni had been playing great together all afternoon. After dinner I played a board game with them, and then we watched TV. They seemed pretty happy.

At 9pm Tahni fell asleep next to me. After I tucked her in, I managed to get Xanthe to bed fairly easily, so I had time to talk to Chris before he fell asleep. I asked him what was bothering him. He was mad that even an appointment to look at a house revolved around Xanthe. I reminded him it was work that had caused me to be unable to go. "Work," he yelled, "that you had to make up because you took off time to be with Xanthe."

I wanted to cry. Instead I promised to go see the house tomorrow. He just shrugged and rolled to his side of the bed.

Sometimes I get so frustrated with him. I have asked him time and time again to come with us, or even just with me, to a couple of therapy appointments so that he could gain a better understanding of what is going on with Xanthe. Each time he refuses, stating that he doesn't believe in that stuff. I have tried to explain this illness to him myself, but I think he feels that my opinions are biased. I understand this totally, which is why I want a doctor to talk to him. I wonder what he is afraid of, why he won't go? With these thoughts in mind I spent another night staring at the ceiling, crying silently, waiting for Xanthe to come in and wake me up.

WEDNESDAY MAY 8TH

~ Chris couldn't get an appointment to see the house yesterday, so he had made one for today at six o'clock. I rushed home from work and made sure everyone was ready. I didn't want to give Chris anything to be mad about. He ended up very angry anyway. Right as he walked in the door, I exclaimed that we were ready. He gave me this puzzled look and said, "We?"

"Yes, we." I stated. "What's wrong with that?"

He became angry and explained to me that the kids were not going. We argued. He didn't want them to go because they were kids, and this was an adult decision. I was mad that he was being so stubborn and childish. I totally felt that this was a family decision. The kids have to live there too! Plus, I knew the real reason he didn't want them to go. It was all part of his power struggle with Xanthe. In the end I left the kids (crying and arguing) with my mom and we went. The entire drive we argued and yelled at each other. By the time we arrived at the house, we had not only agreed NOT to buy the house, but we had decided to break up as well. We did go through the motions though of looking at the house with the realtor. It was a beautiful house. I immediately fell in love with the huge deck. It had a beautiful view of the land. The entire drive home we gave each other the silent treatment.

When we got home Xanthe and Tahni were still mad. I asked them to take a walk with me. I apologized for them not getting to go. I promised them that they could go next time, and I did my best to explain what was wrong with Chris. I blamed the entire thing on stress and his job. They bought my story and forgave him in their minds. I then told them all about the house. They were even more excited now that they could picture the details in their minds.

After dinner I sat on the back porch by myself. I spend a lot of time outside talking to the dogs and praying for answers. Of course, the dogs never give me any advice. I admitted to myself that I was scared. There were so many things that could go wrong with buying a house in the country. We would be so far away from the people I relied on for help. The kids would have to change schools. The country setting would give Xanthe a multitude of new things to worry about. *What is the right thing to do?*

FRIDAY MAY 10TH

~ We took the kids to see the house today. They loved it. It was so cool to see them running from room to room shouting out descriptions and plans. We had been renting and moving around since the divorce 6 years ago, so something permanent was a dream come true for them. By the time we left, they had both picked out bedrooms, Xanthe had designed a 4-wheeling track in his head, and Tahni had chosen the place for the pool. Everyone was happy.

The excitement came crashing to a halt at bedtime. Both kids were upset. Xanthe, because he had decided that his new room was too small, and Tahni, because she didn't want to change schools. She had gone to the same school since kindergarten. I stayed up with both of them, and we brain stormed ideas to solve their problems. For Xanthe, we agreed to consider adding on after a year or two. For

Tahni, I agreed to drive her into her old school every day if I had too. I know it sounds like a dumb idea, but the way I see it is that I have gone to greater lengths numerous times to make Xanthe comfortable, so this was the least I could do for Tahni. Plus her school was only 9 minutes from my work so I was practically going there anyway!

By the time I finally solved all of their problems and got them to sleep, Chris was asleep also (or pretending to be) so I sat up for awhile trying to make some sense of our lives. Everyday something goes wrong or someone needs building up. I try to be everything for everybody, but I fail more than I succeed. If I could somehow cure Xanthe, then I think everything else would just fall into place. If a cure isn't possible, then I am afraid I am going to have to work a miracle to solve my problems with Chris, with the new house, with my job and even with life in general. I would gladly give this responsibility to someone else, but no one seems anxious to take it. *Maybe if I just had a little help?*

MONDAY MAY 13ᵀᴴ

~ The kids went to their dad's over the weekend. I spent the time cleaning, reading and playing on the computer. I always feel nervous when they are gone. I think it is because I am always so busy keeping their lives on track, that when I am alone, I don't have anything to do. Who knows? Maybe eventually, when life calms down I will learn how to live again.

I heard from the kids a few times. Twice it was because Xanthe was upset, and once it was Tahni complaining of being bored. I had no luck with her problem, but I was able to calm Xanthe down both times without having to go get him.

I tried to spend some time with Chris, but he busied himself with other things. Either he really did have things to do or he was avoiding me. In my exhausted, fragile state I chose to believe the latter. I should have just asked him because I was probably wrong. Communication has not been our strong point lately. We both know we should try harder, but we are too exhausted and emotionally drained to give it much effort.

By the time I picked the kids up today, I was totally ready for their company. I think they must have missed me too because we had a great evening together with no arguing or episodes. Bedtime even went fairly well. I was actually able to get to sleep by midnight.

TUESDAY MAY 14TH

~ I was at work when Xanthe's dad called to tell me that the tutor cancelled today. Even though I had a ton of work to do, I called her to explain that we really needed to makeup the time. I explained that Xanthe was due to go on a sixth grade camping trip with his class on Friday, so that only left Wednesday and Thursday for tutoring this week. She agreed to come for three hours both days, but not before she got in a comment about him being well enough to go camping. I didn't even try to argue with her. What she didn't know was that Xanthe's dad was having to go with him so that Xanthe would be able to make it through the trip. No one else was bringing their dad. Xanthe was even going to have to sleep in the same tent as his dad, instead of in the big tents with the other boys. Yeah, he was well enough all right!

By the time I got home, I was mentally exhausted. I was so tired of fighting everyone on everything having to do with Xanthe. I almost ordered out for dinner, but Tahni offered to help me make something and I was eager for some time alone with her. We had a great time in the kitchen by ourselves.

Dinner went OK. Xanthe didn't have any problems with the menu safety-wise, but he did refuse to eat it out of dislike. I made him a couple of turkey sandwiches. Chris jumped at the chance to repeat his lecture on eating what you are served. It always ends with... *that's how my parents did it, and I turned out just fine.* I opened my mouth to blurt out my usual comeback, but decided I was too tired to argue. I just wanted to get through dinner and then head to bed. Luckily bedtime was easy and I got my wish. Asleep by 11pm!

THURSDAY MAY 16TH

~ Tutoring went horribly, both yesterday and today. The tutor was upset that Xanthe could go camping, but couldn't stay awake for her sessions. We didn't bother to argue with her. It was enough for us to know that he would sleep late at camp too, but he would still get up in time to enjoy the afternoon and evening activities. It wasn't his fault that the nightmares kept him up all night, and that the medications made him groggy. I thought about calling the district office again to complain and try to work something out but, in the end I figured it would be useless. We only had a few more sessions left to live through anyway, and none of my prior phone calls had changed anything. I said a silent prayer instead, urging the tutor to stick it out for a few more days.

After a fast food dinner, we spent the evening packing and making not one ,but two last minute trips to the store for forgotten supplies. I am not sure if all that stuff was really on the school's list (a snake bite kit!), but Xanthe insisted he had to have it all, and I just wanted to do whatever I had to, to make this camping trip a success. I think he desperately needs some time with his friends. I do not want him to alienate himself any further than he already has.

Xanthe was very excited about the trip until bedtime. Once he was in bed, Xanthe started to panic about not being able to make it through camp. I kept pointing out that his dad would be there. That didn't seem to be enough for him. By the time he finally fell asleep, we had covered every topic from poisonous bug bites to escaped killers lurking in the woods at camp. It was an exhausting night.

FRIDAY MAY 17TH

~ As I dropped Xanthe off at his dad's this morning, I said a little prayer in hopes of making this weekend turn out right. Xanthe's dad looked a little nervous and scared. I reminded him to call me if things turned bad.

Tahni was excited when I picked her up from school. I could see the smile on her face from across the playground. When she spotted me, she practically ran for the car. As she jumped in the car she screamed, "Yeah, a whole weekend without Xanthe!"

That made me laugh. I understood her excitement though. We had made big plans for this weekend. I wanted to make it special for her and give her some much needed time with me. The entire drive home was filled with a giddy non-stop dialogue of what she was looking forward to the most. I just smiled and listened. It was great to see her this happy.

By the time we had dinner, played a few games, watched a movie and did each other's hair and make-up, Tahni was spent. I could tell from the circles under her eyes that she was ready for bed, but she insisted that she wanted to stay up. My offer of a story, made up by me and starring her, changed her mind, and I finally got her into bed. I rubbed her back as I told the story. She was asleep before I finished the tale, but I stayed with her for a few extra moments just to watch her sleep. A part of me didn't want the evening to end either. It was nice to have a bedtime filled with calm and happiness instead of fear and crying.

SATURDAY MAY 18TH

~ We woke up early and started our weekend with a breakfast composed of foods that Xanthe wouldn't eat. Biscuits and gravy were Tahni's first pick, and we threw in some eggs and fruit for good measure. With our bellies full, we headed off to the store. We had a ton of supplies to buy. Since Chris was going to be working all weekend, Tahni and I had planned a "spa" weekend for ourselves. We even invited my mom. Tahni and I had spent a week making out the list. We laughed and teased each other as we picked out facial masks, nail polish, lotions and even a hair highlighting kit. I said that we should all go red, but Tahni decided on blond!

Our next stop was the grocery store. We bought snack foods and seafood for dinner. Again, all the stuff that Xanthe doesn't want to eat. Mom and I were trying hard to make this weekend all about Tahni, so her tastes ruled. We ended up with an odd assortment of food, but Tahni didn't seem to mind that nothing really went together. Our final menu consisted of stuffed mushrooms and boiled shrimp for appetizers, beef stroganoff as the main course, and tiramisu for dessert. As odd as it sounds, it was awesome!

Once we got started, we had a blast with our spa experience. First, we highlighted each other's hair. Then, we gave each other foot and back massages. We did our nails and we ate our "cool" foods while we watched numerous chick flicks. It was really fun. The best part was seeing the smile on Tahni's face as she drifted off to sleep cuddled in my arms. Sometimes I feel my love for her so strongly that it hurts.

SUNDAY MAY 19TH

~ Today we continued our girlfest until 3pm, when it was time to pick Xanthe up. As the clock sped closer to three, Tahni became more and more rushed in her activities. I think she was trying to cram as much cool stuff into our time together as possible. She eventually wound down, and we spent the last hour cuddling on the sofa trying to fit in some last minute one on one time.

Xanthe was very wound up when we picked him up. At times, he was talking faster than his mouth would work. He had so many experiences to share that it took about three hours to get all of the details out. By the time his story was finished, I felt safe in the knowledge that he had had a good time. There were a few points over the course of the trip where he had freaked out or become sad, but it seemed that his dad and his friends were able to pull him out of it fairly quickly. The nights had all been rough and had involved staying up late racked with fear, but they had weathered them together. All in all, it seemed that the weekend had gone great for everyone!

I wasn't sure how bedtime would go, but it ended up working out fine. Xanthe was pretty worn out and he seemed more relaxed since he was at home. Plus, I had dosed him with Benadryl to help him sleep, incase the stress from the weekend overtook him. After about an hour of rehashing the details of camp yet again, and cuddling with me on the sofa, he was out like a light.

MONDAY MAY 20TH

~ Well today was horrible. I got a call at noon from Xanthe's dad informing me that the tutor had never shown up. I immediately hung up with him and called the school. They informed me that when they had gotten in this morning there had been a fax on the machine from the tutor saying that she had quit. They had assumed that I knew. Confused I hung up and called the district. The supervisor there informed me that the tutor had expressed concern that Xanthe wasn't cooperating and that she was unable to teach him under the circumstances. I started crying right there at work at my desk, in front of everyone. "Did this mean that Xanthe wouldn't graduate?" I asked her.

She sounded sympathetic when she informed me that she was going to tutor Xanthe herself and that he would still graduate. She figured that since there were only a few days left of school, she should be able to step in and finish up his studies and testing. I was devastated. We were behind with the other tutor, but at least she was up to date on the game plan. I expressed my concern with this, and the supervisor assured me that she could catch up. We set up a time for her to come by and then I hung up. I called Xanthe's dad back and told him what I had found out. Neither of us was very comfortable with the situation, but we realized we really had no other choice.

The rest of my day went by in a blur, until bedtime. I was tired, stressed out and worried and Xanthe was hyper. Since he didn't have any homework to do, he spent the evening running around the house devising projects. I threw together something I hoped would pass for dinner, and Chris and Tahni worked on her homework together. We tried watching a movie together, but I couldn't concentrate and Xanthe couldn't sit still. Between the two of us, the movie was interrupted often. Chris had to keep rewinding the tape, and no one could follow the plot. We eventually turned it off and settled for a thirty minute sitcom.

When it was time for bed, Xanthe was still hyper. Chris and Tahni went on to bed, but I stayed up with Xanthe. He sat up playing on the computer all night. I fell asleep on the sofa. He woke me up every thirty minutes or so to show me something he had found or to have me spell something that he needed to type. I begged him to lie down with me, but he was too wired. I have no idea what time he finally fell asleep on the floor in front of me.

WEDNESDAY MAY 22ND

~ The new tutor came by today for her first and last visit. After reviewing the previous tutor's progress sheets, she decided that she and Xanthe would only need one session together. I tried to argue the point with her, but she seemed convinced of its merits. Xanthe handed in all the work the last tutor had given him and then they did a spelling test, a math test and a science test. The visit took about four hours. We will never know how Xanthe did on these tests, but when the tutor called me later, she informed me that Xanthe had passed and that she had turned his grades into the school. I thanked her and hung up, it was too late to be asking questions now. I had to wonder though… *did this mean that Xanthe actually knew enough to pass the sixth grade and be prepared for the seventh, or did it mean that they had graded him on what he had managed to complete and passed him on effort?*

I am really afraid of what the future holds for Xanthe. Just by talking to him and seeing what little homework I could get him to do, I felt that he was nowhere near ready for the seventh grade. Last time he was tested, he was reading at a fourth grade reading level. All of his spelling tests this year resembled Tahni's fourth grade spelling tests. And I knew for a fact, that he was way behind in math. If he manages to go back to school in August for the start of seventh grade, he is going to be way behind. While I sat up with Xanthe tonight during one of his anxious episodes, I tried to imagine what the future held for all of us. I have to admit that I didn't think it looked all that promising.

FRIDAY MAY 24TH

~ Today was 6th grade graduation. The school had called me and expressed their desire for Xanthe to be there. He was still their student, after all. It was odd to see him walk down the aisle with all of the other kids. His entire family clapped with pride when they called his name. I clapped extra hard knowing how rough it had been for him to make it this far. He was all smiles as he sat by his friends throughout the ceremony. I think he was glad for this chance to be back in the group again. I was impressed with and touched by the way his friends joked around with him as if nothing out of the ordinary had happened. It was as if they all just picked up right where they had left off, Xanthe included.

After the ceremony, we went to see the nurse. We had bought her a present to hopefully convey how much we appreciated everything she had done for all of us over the years. It was her understanding, patience and strength that had made it possible for Xanthe (and me) to survive all seven years at school. After much thought and mind changing, I had purchased a gift certificate to a day spa for her. On the card I wrote, among other sentiments, *You have spent seven years taking care of us, now please, go take care of yourself!* She cried when she read it and then gave me a hug. I suddenly felt awkward, even inadequate, like I should have done more. I stood there silently wishing that there was a way to truly express how much she had improved our lives. She had held me up numerous times when I felt like I was falling. Over the last year I had spent more time with her in her office than I had at work. In the end, I just hugged her again and whispered "thank you" through my tears, hoping she could read my mind.

Once outside, we hung out in the parking lot for awhile to give Xanthe some extra time with his friends. Most of the parents said very little to me, but a few that had some knowledge of our ordeal came over to congratulate us on making it through the year. It was kind of awkward, and I didn't know quite how to respond, but I hope I managed to let them know that I appreciated their concern and support.

For dinner, we celebrated Xanthe's graduation with a meal of his choice and the entire evening went well. Xanthe was still in a great mood by 9pm and bedtime went smoothly. As I tucked him in on the sofa and kissed him goodnight, he informed me of how happy he was that he had graduated. I told him I was happy too and proud of him and for him, then I slipped off to bed and left him to fall asleep while watching TV.

THURSDAY MAY 30TH

~ I had mistakenly thought that the end of the school year would reduce our stress. I was wrong. It has been a long week. If anything, Xanthe has been more upset than usual. He is nervous about our up coming move. He is nervous about staying home with just his sister this summer. He is nervous about next school year. Heck, one night he was even nervous about being able to afford his own retirement. I never know what it will be with this kid!

We are tentatively closing on the house next Friday, so hopefully next weekend will be moving day. I have enlisted the help of Chris' sister to hang out with the kids a couple days a week while I work, and I have negotiated a different schedule at work that will allow me to have Wednesdays off. Their dad has agreed to have them on Mondays. I feel prepared, but I am sure I am missing something!

The last few nights have been hard for Xanthe. He has been very down on himself and life, in general, and the nights give him too much time to think, since they are so quiet. I stayed up a few nights with him just to help keep his mind occupied. He seems very depressed. He is sleeping a lot, but when he is awake he is miserable. I have tried everything in my power to reach him, but I can not bring a smile to his face. Chris and Tahni have tried too, but to no avail. I finally convinced him to take a shower today and the whole family was glad. It had been three days since he had moved from the sofa, so it was definitely time.

SATURDAY JUNE 1ST

~ Today was a lazy day. Xanthe was still feeling down and the rest of us were just tired. No one seemed to be in the mood to go anywhere or do anything constructive, so we all puttered around the house, not accomplishing much until dinner time. Xanthe insisted that he wasn't hungry, so the rest of us ate without him. Later, I played cards with Tahni, while Chris and Xanthe watched TV. Xanthe kept dosing off throughout the evening, but he never became upset or agitated.

I assumed that bedtime would be a piece of cake, given Xanthe's state and all, but he had a hard time settling down again tonight. This time, though, his mood was different than the last few nights. He seemed more anxious than depressed. I did finally settle him down around 1am, but he started crying hysterically for me about an hour later. I sat up with him until 5:30. He was very depressed and stuck on one subject for hours. I tried changing the subject numerous times, but it was as if he couldn't hear me. He seemed very out of it. His eyes were only half open the entire time, his breathing was heavy and his pulse was very fast, about 120 to 150 beats per minute. Once he finally fell asleep, I held him and prayed for help. The entire episode scared the hell out of me. I had never seen him look or act this way before. At first, I was afraid that he had had a reaction to the medications, but it had been awhile since we had made any changes. Maybe he is coming down with something or maybe his illness is getting worse.

SUNDAY JUNE 2ND

~ Xanthe was tired most of the day. He wasn't depressed anymore, but he was confused about last night. He claimed he didn't remember being sad and saying all the things I claimed him he said. When I questioned him about them, he stated that he didn't feel that way at all.

All day long, I walked around in a daze of worry and exhaustion. It seemed very odd to me that he didn't remember last night. I was also dreading bedtime for fear of a repeat episode. It was hard for me to get motivated to make dinner. As I sat on the sofa fighting the need to move, I realized how badly this was affecting my relationships with Chris and Tahni. I just didn't have the will to do much anymore. I was less talkative, lazier. My mind was always occupied with the problems at hand, and my body was always craving down time. It was as if I was trying to conserve energy for the long nights ahead. They were both missing out on all the small things I used to do with them and for them. I felt bad about letting them down, but it was so far gone now that I had a hard time coming up with a way to start making it up to them.

Unfortunately, bedtime turned out the same for us. We were up late again. More crying, depression and a rapid pulse. His body kept shaking and his eyes were half closed. I wrapped him in blankets in case he was cold. His breathing was rapid and labored. He seemed out of it, as if he were inches away from passing out. He would space off in the middle of sentences, and he didn't seem to know where he was. The way he was acting scared me. It was just like last night, only worse. I was afraid to let it go too far, incase it was a drug reaction, so I call the psychiatrist. In real time, she called back quickly, but at the time it seemed like hours had gone by before the phone rang. I spent the time trying to come up with a realistic cause for his problems. If it was medication related, it didn't seem right that it only happened in the middle of the night. On the other hand though, he did take different medications at night than he did in the morning. I couldn't image what else it could be. He hadn't been anywhere in a week, he hadn't eaten any new foods. I was around him every minute so it didn't seem logical that he could have gotten into something when my back was turned. With every turn my mind took on the subject I hit a dead end.

MONDAY JUNE 3ᴿᴰ

~ I called in sick to work today. So far they have been very understanding, but it scares me. How many times will they let this happen before they have to take some action? I hate failing. I do not want to disappoint them. I have no choice, though. Xanthe didn't fall asleep until 10am. I was tired also, but I couldn't sleep. I was frustrated and stressed out all day. When the doctor called me back last night, she wasn't too concerned about most of the symptoms but she was concerned about his lack of sleep. She thought we should change his dosing times. I am going to move his Lamictal dose from evening to morning because it can sometimes cause insomnia. Hopefully, this will help, but I am doubtful. The way he was acting last night did not look like insomnia to me. It was way too scary and irrational to be taken lightly.

I did take Tahni to school since she had slept though the entire ordeal. Once home, I started cleaning the house around a still sleeping Xanthe to give myself something to do. It didn't really take my mind off of our problems, but it did make me feel like I was accomplishing something real. I also went on the Internet to see if I could find any insight into these episodes, but I came up empty handed.

Xanthe didn't wake up until five o'clock in the evening. This of course did not sit well with Chris, but he let it slide. When he finally did wake up, Xanthe seemed to be in a "normal" mood. Our evening together went fairly well. We had a quiet dinner, watched some TV and relaxed. Xanthe amazingly was still tired. He dosed and went to bed around 9pm.

WEDNESDAY JUNE 5ᵀᴴ

~ Xanthe was still asleep when I left for work, but Tahni was up and she promised to call me if they needed anything. I should have been off today, but since I called in on Monday I needed to make up the time. I was a little worried because the kids would be home by themselves, but I only heard from them twice and both times it wasn't anything serious.

I came home to find the house pretty calm and the kids playing nicely. It seemed like a good start to a good evening. I even had enough energy to make a real dinner. I smiled when Chris came home and I saw his eyes light up as soon as he smelled the food. My reward for a home cooked meal? A great big hug and kiss!

After dinner Chris informed us that we had received some bad news about the house. The realtor had called to let him know that we couldn't close on the house until next week. Something to do with the house not passing inspection. I was OK with it because it gave me more time to plan, but the kids and Chris were devastated. It wasn't as if we weren't going to get the house, we were just going to have to wait until a few things could be fixed. Xanthe, of course, kept me up late because he was still convinced we had lost the house. I didn't even try to reassure him. I knew it would be useless so I just rode it out. He talked non-stop about his worries and I just nodded until, finally, he wore himself out and fell asleep.

THURSDAY JUNE 6ᵀᴴ

~ Xanthe woke me up a few times last night, but nothing bad like I had expected. I was expecting a repeat of the worries from bedtime, but he was easily calmed down each time and went right back to sleep. He has been very tired for the last three days. He is sleeping most of the night, but he is also sleeping all day. When he is awake, he is very irritable. The entire family is walking on eggshells around him. Another medication change? I am going to call the doctor again to find out. This is so frustrating. He's either very awake and irritable or zombied out and asleep. I miss the boy I used to know.

Work went well today. I worked extra hard and skipped lunch in hopes of making up for all the time I had been preoccupied with Xanthe. At two, I had my three month review with my supervisor. She only had great things to say about my work and effort. She also repeated all the good things she had heard about me from my co-workers. I felt great knowing all of this, but I still felt I had to bring up the Xanthe situation. I am really glad I did. She assured me that she understood, and informed me that she could see no indication of my work slipping because of it. If anything, I was still ahead of the other people that had started at the same time I had. She marked my review papers as "career on track" and we both signed it. I felt pretty proud of myself as I left her office and headed back to my desk.

My call to the psychiatrist netted nothing and I crossed my fingers for an easy night tonight.

FRIDAY JUNE 7TH

~ Xanthe woke up at 6 am this morning. I was just getting ready to leave for work and I was afraid that something was wrong but he was in a great mood. Very hyper, talking a mile a minute.

He called me a few times at work to tell me about his activities and asked me to pick up supplies for his latest projects. He was busy with ideas all day. Even though he was in a great mood, his demands still wore me out. By bedtime, I was ready for him to go to sleep. I dosed him at 8:30pm, but he did not go to sleep until 2am. Obviously, his days of over-sleeping were a thing of the past for a while. He wasn't sad or even irritable tonight, but he was very energetic, and I was too tired to deal with it patiently. I kept begging him to turn out the lights and cuddle with me on the sofa, in hopes that it would make him sleepy. He was too hyper to try though, and I ended up dozing off a few times on the sofa while he jumped from one project to the next. Finally, I went to bed because he seemed ok emotion-wise, and I figured he would probably be up all night. Before I headed off to bed, I made him promise that he wouldn't cook anything, catch anything on fire or do anything I would think was weird. He smiled at that, but promised. As I walked to my room, I knew the promise was useless. He has poor impulse control and doesn't usually think about what he is doing or whether it is right or wrong. The promise made me feel a little better though. Why? I do not know.

I tried to stay awake once I was in bed, incase he needed me, but exhaustion won out and I finally fell asleep.

MONDAY JUNE 10TH

~ Xanthe was very irritable all day, and it just got worse when we found out that we would not be able to move into our new house this weekend either. Xanthe is very excited to move. The new house has everything he could ever want and he is tired of waiting. I tried to reason with him by explaining that it was just one extra week, but he wouldn't believe me. His anxiety over losing the house was worse this time, probably because this was the second time we had had to wait!

Even with Xanthe's irritability, our evening went fairly well. He mostly stayed to himself, and Chris, Tahni and I busied ourselves by making a list of the things we needed (wanted?) to buy for the new house. Tahni wants an above-ground pool until we can get a real one. I want a ton of kitchen, bath, and living room stuff. Chris had the longest list, but all of his stuff centered around the garage.

Xanthe and I were late getting to bed again tonight. He wasn't depressed or anxious so I probably didn't need to stay up with him, but I felt bad, since I had hardly spent anytime with him all evening. For about an hour he watched TV and I watched him watch TV. After he fell asleep, I waited about 20 minutes then I turned out the lights and headed to bed. I wasn't sure if he was going to sleep all night or not, but I figured I had better get some rest while I could.

THURSDAY JUNE 13TH

~ We had a horrible night last night. We had gone out to see the house again yesterday after dinner, and this time we walked out to take a closer look at the pond. We then realized that it must be leaking, because the water level was very low. We saw one of the neighbors and asked them about the pond. We found out that it had always been low and that there were more than likely no fish in it. This devastated Xanthe. His dreams of his own personal pond were gone just like that!

Bedtime was horrible because of this. Xanthe spent hours crying and arguing about what a bad choice we had made with the house. I told him we would have the pond fixed if we could. I pointed at all the things he loved about the house. He wouldn't hear any of it. Finally, after hours of arguing, I just cuddled up next to him and let him complain. I tried not to look at him while I held him. The pain in his eyes and the sadness in his words broke my heart. I felt like a failure. I had come to believe that this house was a great idea. Now, I wanted to scrap the whole thing.

Work today didn't go much better. I spent a lot of time either on the phone with Xanthe or surfing the Internet for everything I could find about leaking ponds. I didn't really learn much more than the fact that whatever we did, it was bound to be expensive. Not good news and definitely not news I wanted to share with Xanthe. Xanthe did his part today by watching fishing programs and calling me with every remote idea they made him come up with.

FRIDAY JUNE 14TH

~ Ok, it's official the house has passed inspection so we can move next weekend. Chris and I will go Tuesday to sign the final papers. I have to admit that even I am excited now that the pond disaster has passed. After I found a chemical that could be added to the water to stop the leaks, Xanthe let the subject drop. I did omit the part about it costing a fortune, but I figured I would fill him in on that detail later.

For dinner, we decided to celebrate our good fortune, and Chris took us all out to eat. Surprisingly, we all agreed on a restaurant instantly. We all picked our favorites from the menu quickly and sat back to wait on the food. While we waited Chris built a tower out of bread plates and salt and pepper shakers. I thought about mentioning proper restaurant manners, but the moment was too good to ruin. It was nice to see us all so relaxed and happy together.

After dinner we drove around for awhile. Chris said he wanted to look at "city life" one last time. As he pointed out every business, he would add a narrative about his experiences there. Half of the stuff he said was hilarious, and I am sure he made most of it up, but the kids were having a blast listening to his stories. It was a great night that ended way to quickly.

News of the move had made Xanthe happy, but of course the happiness did not last through bedtime. For reasons known only to God, Xanthe became convinced that something would happen to our house before we could move in. He asked a ton of questions about tornadoes, earthquakes, heavy rains and flood plains. Who would have guessed that he even knew what a flood plain was?

MONDAY JUNE 17TH

~ Today I actually feel somewhat rested. Xanthe has been in a better mood all weekend. During his hyper moments he is burning off the energy by packing. This has left me with more time to relax. Even with the problems from Friday night we ended up having a great weekend. On Saturday we had decided to celebrate our last weekend in the old house by having everyone over for a barbecue. We had a blast, even though it wore us out. It was nice to hang out with everyone, and it was fun to talk about the new house. We all made plans for the move and everyone offered to help.

Xanthe even had a good weekend sleep-wise. Maybe because of all the excitement or maybe "just because," but he went to bed easily for two nights and only woke up a few times each night!

Work went well today. The kids slept in and their dad came by to pick them up around 11am. I didn't hear from either one of them all day. Because of that, I was able to concentrate and really get some work done. I did take a lunch though, and I used it to scan the comments on the bipolar web site. After thirty minutes of reading, I started feeling better about my life. From what I had read, it was apparent that things could be a lot worse. Other families were having problems with violence from the rages brought on by bipolar disorder, or even trouble with their children that required involvement from the police. I was thankful that we were not in their shoes, and I said a little prayer in hopes that it never got that bad for us.

TUESDAY JUNE 18TH

~ Today we signed the papers and received the keys to the new house. It was a big day for us so we went out to dinner (again) to celebrate. Everything went fine until Xanthe didn't finish his meal, but asked for dessert. I wanted to let it go since we were celebrating, but Chris was mad. All he said though was, "Order what you want. It doesn't matter what I think anyway."

Both kids look at me in hesitation, but I nodded that it was fine. After that moment passed, we went on to have a good time, on the outside at least. On the inside, I was mad. *Why couldn't Chris just talk about these things with me. Why did he have to blurt out rude comments then stay silent for the rest of the evening?* I understood his anger, but I wished that we had better communication when it came to things like this. I know that finding the time to be alone together to work this stuff out was difficult, but I believed that we could pull it off if we really tried.

During the drive home, the kids were happily discussing the move and Chris and I rode in silence. We were both lost in our thoughts. My mind was occupied with the details of the move. Not furniture hauling and driving logistics, but anxiety control, playmate locating and school transitions. I can only guess at what was on Chris' mind.

Thankfully bedtime was easy tonight because we all stayed up to watch a movie, and Xanthe fell asleep in the middle of it cuddled in my arms. All I had to do was lead him to bed.

WEDNESDAY JUNE 19TH

~ Today I officially started packing. I started by making a list

66

while I ate lunch at work. I felt a little overwhelmed as to where to begin. We have a lot more stuff than I had imagined. I had thrown out or given away a ton of stuff, but we still have an enormous amount to take with us.

After dinner, Xanthe and Tahni started packing their own rooms and they finished pretty fast. It was cool to see them formulate a plan for getting it all done. After much discussion, they decided to help each other out. First, they packed Xanthe's room, then they packed Tahni's. They used up a lot of boxes and threw away a ton of trash. By the time they were done, I still hadn't finished the kitchen. I wanted to quit, but I made myself forge on. By bedtime, I had packed three rooms and I was tired.

Since we were all so busy tonight, we didn't really have any problems with Xanthe. I think part of that was because he was using up his manic energy by packing. Since he had something concrete to do, he didn't have time to run around inventing crazy projects.

By bedtime, I was exhausted. Since Xanthe and Tahni had packed up their rooms, I made them a bed on the living room floor. Having Tahni in there with him must have made Xanthe more comfortable because he was in good shape when I headed off to bed. A few times I got up to use the bathroom, and I could hear them laughing and giggling down the hall.

FRIDAY JUNE 21ST

~ Since tomorrow is moving day, we were all busy from right after work straight through to bedtime. There were so many last minute things to do. I ordered a pizza since I didn't want to mess with dinner. Xanthe had been anxious all day and by noon had called me twelve times, so I had left work a little early. I was secretly glad for the excuse to get out of there because I wanted to get a head start on moving.

Xanthe's anxiety seemed to lessen once I arrived home. He did shadow me as I moved around the house preparing the boxes, but he chatted happily and never once became upset.

Tahni was busy talking on the phone all night. She only hung up when she finally found a friend in the neighborhood that could come over and play. She was adamant about hanging out with someone on her last night in town.

Even though we were all exhausted, bedtime turned out to be a nightmare. I think the uncertainty of moving was getting to Xanthe. He has always been bad with any kind of change and this was a big one. He didn't really voice any new concerns. Mostly he was just worried about making friends, his new school and our general safety. All of the things we had been through a hundred times before. I couldn't really see the point in going over my usual reassurances, so I figured that the best plan of action would be to just shut up and listen. We stayed up and talked until about 2am.

SATURDAY JUNE 22ND

~ Today was fun, but busy. I spent most of my time at the old house supervising that end of the move. Tahni stayed with me, while Xanthe and Chris made trips with our stuff to the new house. Thankfully, we had a lot of help, as it was at least a forty minute drive one way. A lot of family and friends showed up to pitch in, and we put their vehicles to good use.

After a quick lunch of fast food, we took a couple of moments to survey our progress. Since we still had a lot to do and most of the blankets and such still had to be packed, we decided to make a couple more trips and then call it a night by staying one last time at the old house. It was kind of eerie since almost everything was gone. Around 8pm, we ate hamburgers on the floor and then played a board game since the TV had been moved. I used all the blankets to set us up one big bed on the living room floor, and Chris and Tahni fell asleep quickly.

Xanthe and I, though, were up late again. This time he was worried about his stuff getting broken, about someone breaking into the new house since no one was there and mostly about how scary this house looked with nothing inside it. Soon his worry turned to sadness. He became nostalgic about all the memories we had made in this house. He started to cry and asked me to hold him. I tried to stay positive by pointing out examples of memories I thought we could make at the new place. This helped some, but not much. Thankfully, he finally fell asleep.

SUNDAY JUNE 23RD

~ We were busy again today. Somehow we managed to get it all done. Well, almost all done. Tahni and I had gone over to the new house with the second to the last load so that we could start putting things away and preparing for bedtime. Chris, Xanthe and Chris' dad went back for the last load, which should have included our bed. We had been saving our bed until last because it was such a huge ordeal. It was a queen size waterbed. The kind with 10 individual tubes of water instead of one big piece. And the frame was just as bad. I had bought it a year ago. It was a beautiful black wrought iron bed frame with a canopy. I had wanted it forever. Unfortunately, each piece had to be taken apart before it could be loaded. By the time they were ready to disassemble the bed, Chris was worn out. He made the crazy decision to just leave it there. Mattress and all. Needless to say, I was very annoyed when I heard the news. Chris tried to appease me with promises of a bigger, better bed, but I was still annoyed. All we had to sleep on were three twin mattresses. Two were the kids and one was an extra. That's four fairly large people and three small mattresses. How was that going to work? We finally decided to push them all together in our room and sleep like that until we bought a new bed.

Once we were all in bed, I realized that I actually liked the new sleeping arrangement. I figured it would work out perfectly while we were getting settled. This way, Xanthe would have time to get used to the new house, while still being next to me at night. Maybe I would be able to get some solid sleep.

TUESDAY JUNE 25TH

~ The drive to work these last two mornings has been a killer. For eight years now, I have never spent more than 10 minutes on my commute to work so to me thirty minutes seemed like an eternity. Adding to that, the fact that I had to get up earlier than usual made the new arrangement a nightmare.

Surprisingly, Xanthe has not had any major problems for the last two days. I had assumed that the first few days would be the hardest, but I guess the newness of it all is still keeping him busy. It helps, of course, that Chris' sisters have been out to spend time with the kids. If it wasn't for them, I have no idea what I would have done.

Chris hates our sleeping arrangement. When he rolled over last night to hold me, he kept touching the kids. I think it is funny, and I have to admit that I do not mind reminding him that it is his fault we have to sleep like this. Secretly I am glad. Xanthe has had a hard time settling down at night. The new house makes strange noises and the country seems open and unsafe to him. With us all in the same room, it makes it easier for me to be with him and still get some sleep. I am contemplating taking my time on picking out a new bed. Maybe I can stretch the whole thing out until Xanthe is capable of sleeping in his own room. Then again, that could take ten years and I think Chris might catch on by then!

On a happier note, we all love the house. Of course, we are far from unpacked, but we are enjoying the room. We hang out on the deck every night. Xanthe rides his 4-wheeler every day and the kids have even made some new friends. I think this may work out after all.

WEDNESDAY JUNE 26TH

~ I received some bad news today. Before we moved, I looked into the area schools. There were supposedly two in our district. After some research, I decided that one was better. I asked the realtor if our kids would be in the district for the good school and he assured me that they would. Of course today, I called the school to start the enrollment process and found out that we aren't in their district after all. I do have a few options, though. I am going to write the school board and request a waiver to allow my children to attend their school. There are 3 other children on our street that attend their school, so I am thinking that the wavier will be granted. If not, I will need to come up with a better plan. I can not send Xanthe to the other school. Because of circumstances with the special education program, ages of attendance and other things, Xanthe would never be able to thrive there. I should have known better than to think the whole school thing would just work itself out! Nothing in our lives ever happens without a battle.

The rest of our day went pretty well. Chris' sister was still over and she and Tahni swam before dinner and then jumped on the trampoline until dark. We all played a board game before bed, and then Xanthe chose to sleep in the living room in his chair since Chris' sister was sleeping on the couch. That gave us more room in our bed, and Chris could stretch out without bumping into Tahni.

FRIDAY JUNE 28TH

~ Xanthe went to his dad's today. Every year he goes to stay with his dad for the week before July 4th. Xanthe's uncle owns a firework stand, and each year Xanthe gets to work there. His uncle pays him in fireworks and a little cash. The Fourth of July is Xanthe's favorite holiday. Every year he takes the fireworks that he has earned and puts on a display for our family and friends. The older he gets the better the displays get. This year Xanthe is especially excited. He has learned a lot over the years and he has big plans for this year's display. I have invited over forty people to come out to the house and watch his show.

I tried to get out of work early today, but we were behind on a deadline and I ended up working 30 minutes late. Because of that, I hit some rush hour traffic that put me behind schedule even more. Once I turned onto gravel, I sped up and eventually pulled into the driveway in a rush because I needed to make up for lost time.

By the time I had driven Xanthe into town to go to his dad's, drove back home and then made dinner, the evening was practically over because of my late start. Luckily, Tahni and Chris were also tired, so we all went to bed early. I knew I was exhausted, but I figured I would have trouble falling asleep since I was usually up with Xanthe every night, so I wanted to get a head start on getting some sleep. My plan back fired though, and after two hours I found myself wide awake, listening to Chris and Tahni breathe and staring at the ceiling. I finally gave up and went back into the living room to read.

MONDAY JULY 1ST

~ The last few days have gone by smoothly. It feels as though we have been pretending to lead a normal life. We wake up, eat breakfast, go about our day then spend the evenings relaxing and hanging out in the back yard. We even had the neighbors over last night to swim and eat. The difference in our days with and without Xanthe is like black and white. There is no arguing, no one is scared, and I do not have to be on the look out for irritability gone bad.

I have had a great time reconnecting with Chris and Tahni, but I am still stressed out. It's like I do not know how to live any other way. My body and mind are in ready mode. Sub-consciously, I am alert to every action, every word, ready to step in, if need be. And my mind keeps wondering to thoughts of Xanthe. I miss him. I call his dad constantly. *Does Xanthe need me? Is he sleeping at night? Is he remembering to take his medications?*

From the reports from his dad, it seems that Xanthe has been doing very well. The days at the stand are wearing him out. He has to load and unload fireworks, price them, set them out for display and wait on the customers. He is totally in his element. During the day, his anxiety is mostly staying at bay. He has had only a few moments that he has needed his dad's help in calming down. But the nights have been bad. Xanthe has gone from scared to grumpy to hyper and back again. His dad is exhausted. When I talked to him today and he retold the story of the troubles with last night, I thought I could hear a hint of tears in his voice. I tried to reassure him and let him know that he was doing a great job, but I know from experience that words don't help. I hung up feeling sad and fighting the urge to go get Xanthe. I had to force myself to let him stay at his dad's for three more days. I knew that by morning he would be glad he had stayed and so would I. One, I needed to let him work this stuff out with others or, even better, by himself. It is just so hard not to rush in and rescue him. Two, I needed this time with Chris and Tahni as much as they needed it with me. We all love Xanthe dearly, but he takes up a lot of our time, and Tahni and Chris were thoroughly enjoying the extra time I was able to spend on them and with them. It was a good change of pace for everyone, Xanthe included.

WEDNESDAY JULY 3RD

~ Tahni and I slept late today, and Chris went to work. I had taken today and Friday off for the holiday weekend. We puttered around the house for awhile just enjoying the quiet.

Around noon, we headed down to the stand to pick Xanthe up. It took an hour to load the car with everything he had gotten for his display. There were some very heavy, very large pieces. Xanthe informed me, very excitedly, that those were the big nighttime pieces for his grand finale. He was very pumped up and he talked non-stop on the way home about how great his display was going to be. As he told the story about his duties with the pricing machine, I realized from his description that his display was worth well over six hundred dollars. I felt a little concerned about driving home with such a large amount of explosives behind me, but we made the trip without any mishaps.

Once we arrived home, we spent another hour unloading the car, and then Xanthe disappeared into his room to draw up a plan for his firework show. He even asked Tahni to help and the project kept them busy for hours.

Once Chris came home, Tahni and I had to sit through another telling of the fireworks story. Xanthe was so excited about the whole thing that I think he would have told it to the mailman if he had seen him when he came by.

By 10pm, Xanthe was still going a mile a minute so I stayed up with him, and Chris and Tahni went to bed. I turned the lights off and lowered the volume on the TV. Eventually exhaustion took over and Xanthe fell asleep in his chair. I tucked him in and headed off to bed, praying that he would sleep all night.

THURSDAY JULY 4ᵀᴴ

~ It's a tradition in my family to go to my uncle's farm for the Fourth of July. He has a big pond, a lot of land and a professional firework show after dark. Tahni had invited a friend ,and they spent the day swimming in the pond and lighting small stuff like sparklers and smoke bombs. Xanthe spent the day fishing and throwing firecrackers into the pond. He hung out with his older cousins and had a great day. Chris spent the day riding his four-wheeler and hanging out with friends. Every time he drove past me, he would swing by and stop to give me a kiss. I spent the day being bombarded with questions about Xanthe and Tahni. Everyone wanted to know what was going on with Xanthe. And they all wanted to offer their advice on raising Tahni. Everyone was concerned that she was having to grow up too quickly. Nothing like a guilt trip for the holidays!

Finally, it was time for everyone to sit and watch the big display. We had set up some lawn chairs and I went to find Xanthe and Tahni so that they could sit by me. Chris was helping with the show so I couldn't sit by him. The entire show lasted about two hours. It was fun for awhile, but soon my mind began to wonder. I kept stealing glances at Xanthe and Tahni every time a firework would light up the sky. I was looking for signs of concern. *Were they happy? What were they thinking? Was I missing something?* I was overcome with a need to hold them. I scooted my chair closer and held both their hands. I was hoping they could feel my love.

When we got back to the house it was late and everyone else headed to bed. We had a big day planned for tomorrow. That was when we were having our own celebration. We were having a cookout, games and of course Xanthe's display. Xanthe and I did not go to bed. He was suddenly very worried about his display. *Would it be good? Would everyone stop lighting their stuff and just sit and watch his? Would people try to light his stuff? Would everyone stay long enough to watch?* He needed it to be dark before he could begin, and he made me promise to make everyone stay even if they were tired. He was very concerned that no one would take his show seriously since he was just a kid. I wanted to cry. *Why couldn't this be easier for him? Why did everything have to worry him in such big proportions?* We ended up staying up until 4am. I couldn't even sleep after he was out because I was dreading tomorrow. *How was I supposed to keep my promises?* Through no fault of their own, no one really understood how important this whole display was in Xanthe's mind. Since he wasn't like other kids, no one understood his desperation. I wasn't even sure I could explain if anyone happened to ask.

FRIDAY JULY 5TH

~ The day started out innocently enough. Xanthe was up with the sun even though he had just gotten to sleep. The excitement of the day was running through his body. While the rest of us were setting up the volleyball net, the horse shoe pit and the lawn chairs, Xanthe was out at the end of the property setting up his display. Everyone started arriving around noon. Everything went smoothly until about 7 o'clock. I was sitting on the deck watching everyone having fun when Xanthe ran past me and headed inside. My mom thought he might be hurt. I knew better. Something was upsetting him. I went in after him to try to set it right again.

I found him crying in his bedroom. He was convinced that everyone was going to want to light his stuff and that no one would watch him. I wanted to scream at someone. *Why did his favorite day of the year have to be so hard on him?* Instead, I sat down next to him and made him promises I hoped I could keep. After about one hour and a million interruptions, I had calmed Xanthe down. He headed back out to light things and everyone cornered me to find out what was going on. Ah, the fun of family gatherings.

The evening ended up going very well. Everyone did stay to watch Xanthe's display. No one helped him unless he asked for it. Chris watched out for him so that he didn't get hurt. I held Tahni as we kept our faces turned toward the sky. His display was awesome and everyone offered his or her congratulations and praise. Xanthe was grinning from ear to ear for the rest of the night. He even fell asleep with a smile on his face. Even though I was exhausted, I sat up for a while on the deck by myself. I was grateful that everything had worked out so well, but I wished that it had been easier to pull off. Before going in I turned my face up toward the sky one last time and asked God for some help.

SATURDAY JULY 6TH

~ For me, today was horrible. As I was cleaning up the kitchen from yesterday's mayhem, I happened to look down at my hand and realized I wasn't wearing my dad's wedding band. After he passed away, my mom wore it on her hand, and then when life became hard for me, she gave it to me to wear for strength and comfort. I wear it everyday. I stood at the sink trying to retrace my steps. I remembered that I had been wearing it before the display. Then it hit me. I had taken it off to wash up a few dishes before Xanthe got started lighting things and I had set it down on the island. From the window above the sink I had seen Xanthe waving for me to come outside, so I dried my hands and left the kitchen. I had forgotten to grab the ring. I glanced over at the island, but the ring wasn't there.

By the time Chris, Tahni and Chris' sister woke up, I had searched the entire kitchen for the ring. Chris' sister had remembered seeing it on the counter, but she couldn't remember when. Everyone helped me look, but we never found it. I hid in the bathroom for twenty minutes and cried.

Eventually, I got up the nerve to call my mom and tell her what I had done. She didn't get upset with me at all. I know it hurt her, but I think she could hear the desperation and sadness in my voice, and she wanted to make me feel better. She assured me that it would turn up. I started crying even harder at the thought that it might never be found. She sounded just like my grandmother when she started talking about fate, and the fact that I would find it if it was meant to be. And if I never found it? Well then, there had to be a good reason. Maybe dad was trying to tell me that I was strong enough to rely on myself now. Or maybe he wanted me to shift some weight over to mom. Mom didn't know for sure what the reason was, but she was convinced that there was one. Unfortunately, I did not share this belief. I searched the entire house twice more and the back yard once before I finally gave up for the day.

For Xanthe and Tahni, today went great even though they were sorry for me. Xanthe was still riding the high from his awesome fireworks display. He and Tahni played together all day. These are the days that make it all worth the effort. As I watched them, first in the pool ,and then later on the trampoline they both looked truly happy. I stood at the window enjoying the sound of their laughter. I felt good inside for awhile, even with the ring disaster weighing on my mind. Of course, I also waited all day for things to go bad. I was tense and apprehensive, holding my breath waiting for the storm. It never came and the day ended well. Xanthe even went to sleep without any problems. I wish I could say the same for myself.

TUESDAY JULY 9TH

~ Last night was the worst night we have had since this entire ordeal started. It began as it always does. It was bedtime and Xanthe was scared. This time he thought someone was in the house waiting for us to go to sleep. I lay down next to him and held him until we both fell sleep. Sometime later a raw scream woke me from my dreams. I turned around and grabbed Xanthe, automatically whispering calming phrases in his ear. He was shaking and sobbing so hard, I could not understand what he was trying to say. Finally, with much effort, I was able to make it all out. He had felt someone run their hand up and down his spine. It took forever, but I finally calmed him down enough to try to go back to sleep. As we lay there in the dark, side by side, he asked me if I would hold him. I had my arm wrapped around him, so I said I already was. "No," he said, "I mean hold me so that no one else can touch me."

His words broke my heart. I was practically lying on top of him. My left arm and leg draped across his body, half my body lying on his, when he started crying again. I couldn't imagine what could possible be wrong now. I cried when he told me. In the smallest, most frightened voice I have ever heard, he said, "How do I know that you are really my mom and not someone pretending to be her?"

If Xanthe can not even be sure in his mind that I am who I say I am, then what chance do I have of helping him? No wonder he is afraid all the time. If the possibility existed in my mind for everything I relied on to be something else, then I would be scared too. What a terrible burden for a child to bear.

I went to work today, but I couldn't get last night out of my mind. I told a few co-workers that I had befriended about last night's events. They just stared at me in disbelief. I had known that they wouldn't be able to help, but I had needed to tell the story anyway.

I called the psychiatrist on my lunch hour and retold the story to her. She was very concerned that his anxiety was getting out of control. She mentioned a new medication that she wanted to try. Abilify. I assured her I would look into it and call her back within the hour if I wanted it called in.

The web site for Abilify didn't look very promising at first. The medication is approved by the FDA for schizophrenia, not bipolar, but it is being used for the latter by an increasing number of doctors. In studies, it is shown to help with delusions -difficulty separating real from unreal experiences- and comes with few side effects. Unfortunately, one of the side effects is anxiety. I decided that the risk was worth it and called the doctor back so that the new medication could be started today.

I slipped his new medication in with his regular night time dose and hoped for the best. I watched him for an hour for any side effects. The only noticeable change was in how sleepy he was. He fell asleep in his chair before bedtime. I helped him to bed and prayed for good results.

THURSDAY JULY 11TH

~ Yesterday and today were fairly calm. Xanthe seemed overly tired, but nothing else seemed different. He had fallen asleep last night pretty easily and I had started to put some promise in this new medication. I was hopeful way too soon.

Last night was a bad night again. This time, Xanthe was convinced that someone was trying to poison us with carbon monoxide. He had the entire thing thought out in his mind. The "bad guys" had come by earlier when we were not at home and drilled small holes in our walls. Now they were back, and they were pumping carbon monoxide into our house with plastic tubing. It did not matter that we couldn't see or find this tubing, to Xanthe it was there. I tried to calm his fears and get him into bed. He was adamant about staying up. He kept pointing out the fact that you die from carbon monoxide poisoning by drifting off to sleep. Since I couldn't change his mind, I decided to play along and hopefully calm him down that way. As the hours wore on, his words became even more desperate. Eventually we ended up sitting on the deck wrapped in blankets. Even though Xanthe was afraid of the dark and afraid of being outside in the open at night, he was more afraid to stay inside a house filled with carbon monoxide. Sleeping in a lawn chair, on the deck, being bitten by bugs turned out to be too much for me, so I just stayed up the rest of the night. Xanthe and Tahni eventually fell asleep. Thankfully, it was summer vacation and neither of them had anywhere they needed to be. I, of course, had to go to work. It took everything I had just to brush my teeth and put on deodorant. I must have looked like hell at work because people I didn't even know were asking me if I was sick.

I though about calling the psychiatrist again, but I knew that it was too early for the new medication to have kicked in. I surfed my favorite web site for awhile, hoping to come up with something there, but again came up empty handed. Finally, I gave up and threw myself into my work. It must have worked because the next time I looked at the clock it was time to go home.

When I arrived home, I could immediately tell that something was different. Xanthe was sitting in his chair, but his eyes were not focus on the TV. He looked stoned. I asked him how he felt and he was very slow to reply. It seemed as though he had to search for each word before he spoke it. And as the words came out, they seemed to be said in slow motion, maybe even slurred. I was scared enough to call his doctor. She told me to keep an eye on him, and call her if he got worse.

Bedtime was easy tonight. Xanthe was so out of it that he fell asleep as soon as his head hit the pillow. I was thankful for that part, but wasn't sure I wanted to pay the price for it.

SUNDAY JULY 14TH

~ For the last few days, Xanthe has been very out of it. As he walks around the house, he bumps into things. When he reaches for things, it is painfully slow. He stumbles as he walks. His eyes are unfocused and his speech is slow. Just looking at him scares me.

Today he had a bad experience in the shower. As he closed his eyes and put his head under the water to rinse his hair, he felt someone touch his back. I was in the other room folding clothes when I heard the blood-curdling scream. Luckily, Xanthe had stopped locking the door long ago, so I was able to burst right in. I stayed on my side of the shower curtain to talk to him and let him know I was there. I handed him a towel and he got out, even though he still had shampoo in his hair. Eventually he calmed down, and we finished rinsing his hair in the bathroom sink.

All evening I was affected by what had happened. *Was it possible that we would come to a point where he couldn't even shower on his own?* I had to fight the urge to follow him every time he walked out of the room. Things seemed to happen more often when no one else was around, and I didn't think my heart could take another scream like the one I had heard today.

By bedtime, I had given up. The only thing this new medication was helping with was sleep. I would rather sit up with him all night, every night, than watch him struggle to control his speech and movements. Plus, the medication was doing nothing to get rid of these horrible delusions.

TUESDAY JULY 23RD

~ It's been awhile since I have written. Life has been crazy. The same. I was discouraged for a few weeks when the medication wasn't working. The day we stopped the Abilify, Xanthe went back to his normal self. No more stoned movements.

I should have written down the events of the last few days, but they seemed to be repeats of all the days before. I became depressed when I tried to write and ended up reading what I had already written. That just made my bad mood worse.

I do want to write down the details of my battle with the school board, though. Hopefully, I can remember it all. I left off where I had e-mailed the superintendent asking for a wavier to allow my son to attend their school even though he was out of district. The start of school is getting close and I have not heard anything from them, so today I sent another e-mail to the superintendent and one to the head-counselor of the school. A part of me believed this would work. If they have kids, then they will understand the importance of this, and they will not want to cause him any pain. If it doesn't work, I do not know what I will do. I have to get him into that school.

On a better note, Xanthe went to sleep just fine tonight. We had rented another movie and turned out the lights to watch it. This is my new favorite trick. I dose him about 30 minutes into the movie and wait for it to work it's magic. The combination of his medication, the dark, the quiet and the movie plot to keep his mind occupied works almost every time. I am thinking that I should buy stock in my satellite system. I rent a ton of movies from them.

I used the movie time to cuddle first, with Chris, and then with Tahni and to relax. I do not even remember what we watched, but I did enjoy the quiet time.

THURSDAY JULY 25TH

~ Good news for a change. We went to go look at the elementary school and Tahni fell in love. It is a much bigger school than her old school and they have more programs to choose from. Now, both Xanthe and Tahni are sold on the idea of changing school. Yeah!

Our good fortune took a nose dive at dinner tonight. After we were all situated around the table, Chris innocently announced that my cousin had found a 1969 Chevelle that he was looking to buy. Xanthe immediately started in with the questions. This was his dream car. He wanted to know everything about it. The type of engine, the color of paint, the ratio of the rear end, the shift pattern and so on. I looked up when I heard a crack in his voice. He was near tears. I hurried through dinner and then made up a story about needing Xanthe's help in the garage. I asked him what was wrong. He started crying. For the rest of the evening, Xanthe was stuck in a mood of hopeless depression. He was convinced that he would never find another car like that one. He needed to have that car. He insisted that all of his future happiness depended on it. He tried to convince me to go buy the car before my cousin could. I explained that that was not only ridiculous, but also mean. You couldn't buy a car out from under your own family. He cried harder. I tried harder. It was a viscous circle. We spent hours in this mode. He kept slipping further down and I kept holding tighter. In the end, I promised that we would go look at the car. Stupid, I know, but my heart couldn't take much more. It didn't matter, though. Xanthe was already deep into his feelings of gloom, so even that promise couldn't draw him out. I gave him Benadryl at bedtime and held him until he fell asleep.

FRIDAY JULY 26TH

~ Work went well today. I only heard from the kids twice and both times it was Tahni. She was bored because Xanthe was still asleep. Other than that, I had very few interruptions, so I managed to finish up early and I left around 2pm. I was in a hurry to get home and see what kind of mood Xanthe was in. After last night, I was afraid of what I might find.

Xanthe woke up late and immediately picked up where he had left of last night. Sad, depressed, unmotivated. He moped around the house all day. No matter what I did, I couldn't get a smile out of him. Every topic I brought up, he turned around into a discussion about the car. I was desperate to get his mind off of that stupid car, but it was useless. It was so hard for me to understand his fixation. After all, he is only twelve years old. What does he need a car for anyway?

He hadn't eaten all day so I expected him to be starved at dinner time. He wasn't. He refused to eat, even though I had made his favorite meal.

After dinner, Tahni and I tried a few times to engage Xanthe in some activity, but it was useless. Eventually, we gave up and decided to play a board game by ourselves. I was hoping that when he saw the fun we were having he would want to join in, but our laughter didn't faze him. He spent the entire evening with his eyes glued to the TV.

Bedtime was the same, only this time the Benadryl didn't work. We sat up until 2am watching TV, while Xanthe predicted bad things for our future. The infomercials that he usually laughs at didn't faze him at all.

SATURDAY JULY 27TH

~ Different day, same scenario. Xanthe was still in a funk. I tried everything I could think of. I offered to take him fishing, Chris offered to take him 4-wheeling, I even offered to take him to the store to buy him something. He wasn't interested in any of it. His friends called all day, but he refused to talk to them. All he wanted to talk about was that stupid car. If I did get him to move on to a different subject, it was just as bad. It seemed that my only choices for conversation with him included the car or the dismal state of our future happiness. Not much of a choice!

In a desperate effort to at least get him to move from his chair, I tried to convince him to take a shower. His reply, "Why? It doesn't matter. Nothing does."

He ended up sleeping on the sofa off and on all day. None of us knew what to do with him. I couldn't wait for this day to end. If things didn't get any better, I was planning to call the psychiatrist on Monday.

Bedtime was surprisingly easy. I was expecting another night filled with depression and gloom, but at 9pm Xanthe asked for his medication, sunk deeper into the sofa and promptly fell asleep. Tahni, Chris and I stayed up, but none of us made much effort at conversation. Eventually, we headed of to bed. I led Xanthe, still half asleep, to bed and didn't hear from him once.

SUNDAY JULY 28TH

~ Chris, Tahni and I woke up fairly early, and I made us a big breakfast. I thought about waiting for Xanthe or even waking him up to eat, but I was afraid of his mood, so I let him sleep in.

Miracle of miracles, Xanthe woke up around noon in a great mood. He no longer cared about the car. He was hyper and full of energy. He wanted to do everything at once. We were all exhausted from dealing with his depressed mood for the last three days, but none of us wanted to ruin this change for the better. His smile was heart warming and his enthusiasm was contagious.

Since we were all home, we decided to do something as a family. After a short discussion, we decided that we would go to the movies and then out to lunch. Both Xanthe's pick. Tahni and I were afraid to do anything to ruin Xanthe's positive outlook. Chris, thankfully, was playing along. On the drive to the theater I realized how crazy this all was. I truly believe that Tahni and I would have agreed to anything Xanthe chose today just to keep him happy. *What kind of a life is that? What has this illness done to us?*

Bedtime was better tonight, but bad in it's own way. Instead of staying up until 2am dispensing words of gloom, Xanthe kept me up with his hyper activities and words of action. Tonight he invented a system that would allow your car to sense when the windows were icing up and automatically start defrosting them an hour before you woke up. I have to admit the idea does have merit. Tomorrow he wants me to call the Ford people and pitch his idea. How am I going to get out of this one?

TUESDAY JULY 30TH

~ Today was one of those days that mothers live for. After I came home from work, Xanthe and I were lying on the trampoline searching for shapes in the clouds. Tahni was nearby splashing in the pool. Suddenly, Xanthe rolled over to face me and said, "Thank you Mom. I love you. You are the only one who understands me. You are the best mom ever!"

I cried. That startled Xanthe, and I saw panic begin to spread across his face, so I smiled and hugged him and told him that he had just made me the happiest mom alive!

After enjoying the moment a little longer, I convinced Xanthe to get in the pool. Tahni had been begging us to join her for over an hour. Once I managed to get used to the cold water, the kids showed me a game that they had made up earlier in the summer and we played it until dark. It was actually really fun. I was enjoying the ease with which we were relating and I didn't want the evening to end. The smiles, the laughter, the easy going teasing… it was all so perfect. A Kodak moment, as they say.

Thankfully, bedtime was not a battle. Xanthe was a little uneasy, but after a dose of Benadryl and about an hour of cuddling in front of the TV, he was ready for bed. Even though he was still very awake when we headed to bed, he seemed to settle down very easily and I heard very little from him all night.

THURSDAY AUGUST 1ˢᵀ

~ We had another psychiatrist appointment today. I got the feeling that even she was at a loss as to what to do about Xanthe. That scared me. *If she can't help who can?* I asked a ton of questions about different medications I had read about, about different combinations I had heard of, and about different things I was willing to try. By the end of the session, we had decided to start him on Lithium. A large percentage of children are started on Lithium from the start, but it does have some serious side effects. The chance of toxicity was the major reason she had not tried Lithium therapy with Xanthe before. With all things considered though, she was getting desperate, so we agreed to try it. Another draw back to Lithium therapy was the numerous blood draws the patient had to have to check their serum lithium levels. These blood draws were the only way to regulate the levels to avoid the toxicity. The blood draws were not going to be a problem for Xanthe, though. Since I had been drawing other people's blood for so long, my kids were used to the idea. I had even drawn Tahni and Xanthe's blood at one point, and they claimed that they didn't even feel it. Thankfully, this was one thing that Xanthe was not afraid of!

I filled the prescription on the way home, but I was not going to give him his first dose until morning. Xanthe knew about the new medication, but not about it's side effects. I try to hide as many of those from him as possible. Since he is already prone to anxiety attacks, any information he receives of problems concerning his medications immediately freaks him out. I find it best not to give him any ammunition for his already overly-active imagination. The last time he overheard a discussion of side effects, he freaked out for over an hour, convinced he was going to die. And that discussion was only about the chance of headaches and vomiting. Bedtime was long and drawn out. Xanthe kept asking me questions about his new medication. Ever since that disaster with the Abilify, he had become resistant to change. I answered most of his questions honestly, but I could tell that he thought I was leaving something out. I didn't give in though. I had nothing to gain by sharing the side effect information with him. Eventually, he gave up questioning me and fell asleep on the sofa. Once again, I led him to bed and tucked him in with a prayer.

MONDAY AUGUST 5ᵀᴴ

~ The superintendent e-mailed me today. His reply stated, "I have e-mailed your request to the board members. I do not anticipate a change in their policy. The district has received several inquiries about students' attendance from across the state line. Only those students that have been grandfathered in are attending our school at the present time."

School starts in 9 days. I felt that I was no closer to getting the kids into the better school than I was before. I broke down and cried, then I dried my tears and wrote a reply:

> *Dear Sir,*
>
> *I appreciate your effort in this matter; however, I feel I may not have made myself clear. I do not wish to switch districts "just because." My son has legitimate medical problems that make it impossible for him to attend the school in our district. A large reason for this is that he will be attending school with juniors and seniors. We all know that children can be cruel, and because of my son's condition, he will most likely be teased and maybe even harmed. This, of course, would cause the school to be an unsafe place for a child with Bipolar Disorder. Eighteen-year-old boys can harm a twelve-year-old boy both physically and mentally. Also, my son experiences a large amount of stress and anxiety. He knows that the other students may not be as kind as other kids his own age sometimes taunt him. He is very afraid of the "older, bigger" kids and this is causing him an enormous amount of distress. He already knows that he is different,*

and his life is harder than most, but he wants to try and he wants to succeed. As his parents, and as a school official, I would assume that we all want what is best for him, and we all want to give him the chance to achieve his potential. This can only be done at your school. At the other school, they do not have a separate classroom for Special education classes. This means that when my son has a panic or anxiety attack, it will happen in front of all of the other kids. At your school, he will have the option to "get away from" the other kids,while he pulls himself together. My son is very scared right now, but by talking to and befriending the kids we live by, he feels that he can attend school. The neighborhood kids have informed him about your school and he feels more comfortable knowing some of the ins and outs. We do not live by anyone going to the other school, so he has been unable to meet those children or learn about that school.

Because of his medical condition he will be unable to attend school if he has to attend the other school. This is not just the opinion of his parents, but of his medical team, as well. When we first moved here in June, I had every intention of sending him to the school for our district, but as I learned more about their program, their age range and their special education experience, I realized that their school would not work for my son. Because of his medical condition, he needs special support. I do not want special treatment from the school board "just because." I need this wavier for my son's health and his academic future.

A child with bipolar disorder is seriously ill, until stabilized with medication and therapy. Even with stabilization, the opportunity exists for a relapse. When a bipolar child is not given the right environment, then the chance of suicide increases dramatically. So, in essence, the wrong school, and with it a hostile, frustrating environment, could cause my child or any bipolar child to attempt to take his/her own life. So, my request for this wavier is a serious life situation, made necessary due to a medical illness. The right environment and resources are a serious determining factor in a bipolar child's success. Please take some time to rethink your decision. The simple decision to allow this wavier could make all the difference in the world in my son's life and in his future. Please reconsider.

If you need any more information, please feel free to call or e-mail me. And again, thank you for your time, effort and consideration in this important matter.

I spell-checked, grammar-checked, said a prayer and hit send.

WEDNESDAY AUGUST 7ᵀᴴ

~ I still have not heard from the superintendent and I am getting nervous. I had to promise Xanthe that he was going to their school just to calm his ever-increasing anxiety. I was desperate. I called the school to see when the next school board meeting was, but there is not one scheduled until after the school year begins. So, since I could not plead with them in person, I decided to write a letter to the school board members myself, instead of relying on the superintendent to do it:

Dear School Board members,

I have recently been in e-mail discussions with your superintendent regarding my request for a wavier to allow my son to attend your school, instead of the one in our district, due to his medical condition. Since, school is starting very soon and my request is in the process of being denied, I wanted to make one final plea for my son's sake. I would attend a school board meeting and do this in person, but there is not a scheduled meeting until after school begins. Below, I have included the most recent correspondence between your superintendent and myself. I beg you to seriously consider my request. The academic success and general health of my son depends on it. He has had such a hard time since his diagnosis, and we are just now making some progress. He is excited to attend school like a "normal" child, and he is making improvements in all areas of life. He is not, however, capable of attending school in an unsuitable environment. Anxiety is a large part of bipolar disorder. So much so, that it can impair his ability to live a "normal" life. The anxiety he will suffer if he does not have the adequate resources and a non-threatening environment, will cause him to relapse into severe instability. We have fought for four long years to reach this stage. Please give him the chance to get better, to make friends, and to go to school like everyone else. Getting him well means the world to both of us. Please help us achieve this.

As I have previously stated to your superintendent, I will pay out of district tuition. I have talked to my neighbors and they do not have a problem with this exception, and I can provide medical back up for all of the situations stated above.

Thank you very much for considering this request. I appreciate all the time and effort you are putting into helping my son and me. I hope we get to work together this school year.

I made eight copies of the letter, signed each one and mailed them out. I prayed that the letter would help. I was very scared.

THURSDAY AUGUST 8TH

~ Today started out ok, but ended terribly. I went to work as usual, and the kids went to a nearby water park with their aunt. Everything was going well until Xanthe's anxiety got out of hand. His stomach started hurting, he started panicking and then he started crying. Their aunt tried to call me at work, but I had already left for the day. She finally got a hold of me at home one hour later. By this time, Xanthe was curled up in a ball on a lawn chair and very upset. I could tell by the tone of her voice that he was ruining everyone's fun. She didn't think it would be right to make everyone else go home just because Xanthe was scared so she wanted me to come get him. I live an hour away from the water park. I told her I would meet her at the gate. I was upset the entire drive. Chris was mad because his sister had told him what was going on when she couldn't reach me. This whole situation embarrassed him and made him angry. His anger, of course, was upsetting me. I was also upset thinking about Xanthe sitting there completely scared and having no one to comfort him or to understand him. By the time, I arrived my stomach hurt and I had a headache. It took awhile, but by the time we arrived home I had calmed Xanthe's fears. Once he was calm, I tried asking him about what had happened, but he had no insight to share with me. He didn't seem to know what had caused it, and he supposedly had no warning that it was coming on. Since I can not read his mind, I can not figure out how to help. This just adds one more item to the list of things Xanthe is unable to do now that his illness is getting worse.

FRIDAY AUGUST 9TH

~ Today I want to give up. I wish that I could just go to sleep and wake up five years from now. I am tired of trying. The school board has turned down my request for a wavier. I am devastated. Don't these people have children? Don't they realize how important this is to my son's life? We try so hard to get ahead, but every turn throws us a curve ball. Will there ever be a time when all of our hard work pays off? Will we be able to hang in there long enough to see it if that time ever comes? What am I supposed to do now? Send him to the other school? Home school him? Move? Lie? It seems so unfair since I know for certain that at least 10 other children are attending that school out of district. Why couldn't they just slip us in?

I wish I could see the future then I could be sure that I was making the right decisions. I have decided to rent an in-district address from my cousin. I do not plan to live there every day. Some days we will stay with Chris at our old house. This is lying, in a way. Yes, I pay rent. Yes, it is in district. No, I do not sleep there every night. In my commitment to put Xanthe in a safe school and get him well, am I ignoring my values? What am I teaching my kids? Do what you have to do to get what you want? I am so confused, and so scared. I wish someone had the answers.

Work was horrible because I couldn't concentrate. My every thought was on the problem of school. Eventually, I just packed up my stuff and headed home early. I planned to go in early Monday and make up the time. Maybe I would even stay late for good measure.

By bedtime, I hadn't told the kids about my plan yet. I am sure that the idea will raise Xanthe's anxiety level to unheard of heights. I am not sure how Tahni will react. I need a day or two to figure out how to approach this. I also want a chance to talk to Chris about it. Maybe he has some fresh ideas.

SATURDAY AUGUST 10TH

~ I took Xanthe to his dad's today to spend the night and Tahni and I had another one of our Mother-Daughter days. We try to plan these as often as we can to give us some time alone and some time to just relax and reconnect. Last time, we went to the mall and painted ceramics then saw a movie. This time we went to eat at a new Italian restaurant and then to a craft store to pick up supplies to make mosaic tiles. We had a great afternoon. The tiles were messy and hilarious, and the meal was awesome. We laughed, shared a plate of seafood pasta, drank a lot of pop and ordered two desserts. By the time we got home, our pants were too tight and our stomachs hurt from laughing so much. The evening was spent sitting on the sofa and relaxing. We cuddled a lot. We offered Chris our leftovers, but he doesn't like seafood.

The older Tahni gets, the more I realize how much we have in common. I always knew that Xanthe and I connected on a deep level because we share a lot of the same personality traits and thoughts, but lately it has become obvious that Tahni and I share a lot of the same thoughts too. I love that we think alike, like the same foods, share the same tastes in activities and movies and we both like to try new things. When we are alone together, we get to do some really fun stuff that we wouldn't be able to do if we were with others. We make a great team and I am thankful for it.

I told Chris about my idea for getting around the wavier today. After talking to him I felt a million times better. He always looks at things in a matter of fact way, while I get all caught up in the imagined what ifs. He thinks that I have decided to do the right thing. While he still doesn't understand why Xanthe has problems going to school, he does agree that Xanthe could never survive at the other school.

SUNDAY AUGUST 11ᵀᴴ

~ Tahni went to join Xanthe at her dad's for the night. I was tired and depressed. I tried to talk to Chris, to get some outside reassurance that I was doing the right things. What I needed tonight more than anything was a hug and someone to take the weight off of my shoulders for awhile. We ended up arguing instead. It always turns out this way for us. This whole deal is a constant fight for us. Ninety percent of the time I am left to handle all of these situations on my own. Part of this is his fault, he doesn't know what to do so he just closes up inside himself, and part of it is my fault, my life is harder when he is angry so I try not to bother him if I can help it. Now, to make matters worse, we discussed how I may be losing my job. With

Xanthe getting worse I am finding it harder and harder to stay all day at work. I am afraid this is just going to get worse once school starts instead of better. Chris hinted he might leave me. I was too tired to care.

In desperation, I picked up the phone looking for an understanding ear and realized I had none. I was tired of burdening my mom and sister. And what few friends (hmm, they are really just acquaintances) I did have, did not understand what I was going through. So, I retreated to the shower instead. I cried the entire time. Usually that helps, but today I couldn't snap out of it. In desperation, I called Roger long-distance. He used to be my mother's boyfriend, now he feels like family to me. He is like a second father. "Hi, I need someone to cry to…" I said.

We talked for almost 2 hours. He listened, but didn't judge. He told me he had no answers. I told him I wasn't looking for any; I just needed someone to listen. He did have some great advice though about doing my best. He told me to get a huge bucket and put a rock in it. Then I was to pick the bucket up. Then put the bucket back down and add another rock. Then pick the bucket back up again. I was to keep doing this until I put a rock in and couldn't lift the bucket, no matter how hard I tried.

'Then", he said, "Take that last rock out and keep it. That is the rock that shows you your best. You tried with everything you had, but you couldn't lift the bucket because you didn't have any thing left. That's all anyone can ever ask of you. That's your best! And there is never any shame in doing your best, no matter what the outcome."

As soon as I hung up, I got that bucket. I felt a little silly, but I went through the motions of the entire exercise. My neighbor was outside and he kept looking over at me as I filled my bucket. I could tell by the way he looked at me that he thought I had finally lost my mind, but I didn't stop to explain and he never asked. Eventually, I filled the bucket up and found my last rock. I liked the idea of having this rock; this reminder that my best is the best I can do. I wrote "Best" on it in big black letters. Let's hope it helps.

MONDAY AUGUST 12TH

~ We had a psychiatrist appointment today. I left work a little early and met Xanthe, Tahni and their dad at her office. I told her again about his anxiety, about how he can't sleep without having nightmares and about how he sees, hears and feels things I do not. I begged for help. She suggested yet another medication change. This time she wants to add Risperdal. I felt let down. It seemed as though it was just one medication change after another with no real improvement along the way. And medications take time to work. We left knowing that yet again, we were just going to have to play the waiting game.

Chris was in a better mood today. Maybe he had found some time to work through his frustrations. He kissed me when he came in from work and whispered in my ear that it would all be ok. People ask me all the time why Chris and I have never married. This day explains my theory perfectly. Chris has proposed, I wear his ring and he would set a date in a heartbeat, but I love things just the way they are. I love the fact that Chris comes straight home every day because he wants to. He could leave us at any minute if he really wanted to. He has no paper tying him here, the kids are not legally his, and he could disappear from our lives without any legal or monetary repercussions. But he chooses to stay. That is what makes it all so beautiful to me. Chris chooses to come home every day simply because he loves us. No one makes him stay and work through the tough times, he does it because he can't imagine life without us, he does it all for love. I am the envy of a lot of our friends. My "husband" passes up time with his friends, because he is in a hurry to get home to us. Other "wives" have to beg their husbands to come straight home after work. I guess that is why I never really panic when we are arguing. I know deep down that we are both in this for the long haul because we want to be. This arrangement feels stronger and more real to me because it is based on emotion, not on a piece of paper. I know he truly loves us.

Bedtime was crazy tonight. Xanthe is becoming more anxious the closer the start of school gets. I was up with him half the night going over all the possibilities that school held. I tried to only point out positive things, but Xanthe kept bringing up the negatives. Eventually we came up with a plan that worked for both of us. He was asleep shortly after that.

WEDNESDAY AUGUST 14TH

~ Well, school starts tomorrow and it would be an understatement to say that Xanthe is anxious. I had hoped that the medication change from Monday would have kicked in a little by now. I know, wishful thinking. Tonight he was scared. Scared of the unknown. Will he be able to stay? Will he "freak out" in front of his new classmates? Will he make friends? Will his locker open? Will four minutes be enough time to make it from class to class? Things that "normal" kids are afraid of sure, but with this illness his worry is magnified by 100. He wanted me to hold him, he was crying, my heart was breaking. "Please Lord," I silently pleaded for the millionth time, "help my little boy."

Against my better judgement, I have decided to call in sick to work tomorrow. I have a feeling that tomorrow is going to be hell. I think I need this day to help Xanthe settle in and ensure that he stays at school. Plus, the first day is only a half day, so I would have had to leave work early anyway. I didn't tell Chris or the kids about my plans to call in. On the off chance that all went well and I ended up going in after all I figured that I wouldn't have to tell Chris about it at all. That would save one argument. I didn't tell the kids because I didn't want to plant the thought in their minds that tomorrow might not go as planned.

By bedtime, we were all nervous, but Xanthe was the only one expressing his concern. Two hours and a million promises later, he finally fell asleep.

96

THURSDAY AUGUST 15TH

~ At six o'clock, the morning started with fear and tears. I was expecting all of it. Xanthe had been up and down all night with his anxiety and tears. I gave my usual pep talk. I pointed out all the positives of going to school. I looked in his eyes. I could see that he wanted to go, but I also saw the fear he was trying so hard to overcome. To try and ease his fears, I promised to sit in the school office all day. That helped a little, but not much. Helpful? Hurtful? I will never know. All I have learned in the past 5 years while dealing with this illness is that I love him, I will do all I can for him, and that I don't want my little boy to hurt.

Once at the school, we checked in at the office and I informed the staff of my plans to stay. I could tell by their looks that they thought I was a pushover, an over protective mom. I had seen that "this mom is way off her rocker" look a million times before.

I sat down in a chair by the window with a book while the office staff glared at me. My anxious son headed off to his first class accompanied by a paraprofessional. His lips were moving. He was silently repeating the mantra we had made up to help him relax. My lips were silently moving too, only my mantra was *Please, someone help my little boy*.

The bell rang to signal the end of first period. I shifted in my seat. Within seconds, my little boy was opening the door to the office. I searched his face. He seemed to be holding it together. He said he wanted to give me his science book. I knew that he just needed reassurance that I was still here. I smiled, took his book, and told him I was proud of him. Off he went to his next class. I settled back into my chair and pretended to read my book.

Second bell. I wondered if I would see him then. While I pondered that question he came bursting through the office door. Fear was on his face; his hands were shaking. I knew better than to try to talk it out right there. It was taking all he had not to burst into tears. I explained to the secretary that we were leaving for the day and would be back tomorrow. Her look spoke volumes, but I stayed strong. This was about him, not me.

This day was both good and bad. Good because Xanthe made it through two periods, bad because the school was upset with us. Xanthe was anxious again. I had to talk him into going tomorrow. Tonight will probably be another night with no sleep. Plus to add to my stress, I lied to Chris. I told him that Xanthe had made it all day. We argue a lot about Xanthe and I did not have the energy to do it today. My life is one big battle. I battle to understand Xanthe, I battle to be a good mother to my daughter, I battle the school for understanding and help, I battle Chris for support and understanding, I battle family that doesn't understand, I battle brazen strangers with "helpful" opinions, I battle fatigue and I battle guilt. Some days I battle just to breathe.

FRIDAY AUGUST 16ᵀᴴ

~ We had a bad morning, again. I repeated the pep talk. Prayed. Then I promised him that I would again sit in the office all day. He seemed better knowing that I would be there. While he finished getting ready for school, I called in sick to work again. They were not happy. I am out of paid time off. My boss said we needed to talk. I said I would be in on Monday.

First hour and second hour went fine. After he headed off to third hour the counselor and special Ed teacher approached me. "You are being his crutch," they said. "You need to leave; we can't have you sitting here."

On and on they talked, thinking they were helping or just not understanding or both. I did not want to leave. Things were going so well. I fought back tears. Finally, I agreed to wait in the parking lot. I headed outside with a heavy heart and a sense of impending doom.

The school called about forty minutes later and informed me that Xanthe was crying uncontrollable. We had changed plans and he didn't know it. He was doing great until he walked by the office and didn't see me. I know he could have made it all day, but now... well, now it is ruined. We have given him something to be anxious about and broken his trust. Can we recover?

The ride home was horrible. We had stayed at the school long enough for me to calm him down. Once in the car, he instantly became upset again and started in with the questions. *Why did you leave me? Why did you break your promise? Why was everyone so mean?* I tried to interrupt, to explain my side, but he never paused long enough for me to get a word in. *Mommy, I was so scared. Where were you? I hate that place. Please don't ever leave me again!* Finally, he paused for a breath. I saw my chance and went for it. Quickly, I explained what had happened. Every detail. Then I promised that it would never happen again. I apologized for doing the wrong thing and then promised to stay with him next time, no matter what. By the time I had finished my desperate monologue, he had calmed down considerably, maybe even forgiven me.

Once home he was worn out. He sat on the sofa to watch TV, but soon fell asleep. I sat next to him and cried. *What have I done?*, I berated myself silently, *Why did I chance breaking his trust that way? Why didn't I stand up to those teachers and fight for my son? What was I supposed to do now?*

SATURDAY AUGUST 17TH

~ Last night was terrible. Xanthe woke up numerous times calling out for me. Each time he was yelling, "Mommy, where are you?"

It was heartbreaking even though I knew where the anxiety was coming from. Each time I did my best to console him, but he never completely stopped whimpering and his sleep continued to be restless.

Surprisingly, both kids woke up in a fairly good mood today. I sat down to write in my journal while they played, but got caught up in reading my past entries instead. I realized by reading them that our lives had become quite strange. It is just one drama after another. The illness and the medications do weird things to my son, my daughter is stressed out and confused half the time, my relationship with Chris is falling apart, Xanthe is getting worse and I am sure I have lost my job. Our lives seem surreal compared to everyone else's. I try to keep a positive attitude for Xanthe and Tahni and Chris to draw strength from, but inside I am falling apart. Sometimes I sit outside on the deck and imagine what it must be like to live in other people's houses. *What do they do all day? How do you fill the time when life is relatively normal?*

Bedtime was uneasy. Xanthe was too keyed up to attempt sleep, so we stayed up late watching TV. I was exhausted, but feeling too guilty to abandon him again. Tahni fell asleep next to me on the sofa. Eventually sleep overcame Xanthe too, and I quietly led him to bed.

SUNDAY AUGUST 20TH

~ I am crying as I write this. I hate our life. I am almost ready to give up my belief in God. *Why does my son have to suffer so much? Why can't it be me instead? What did he ever do to deserve so much pain? He is such a good kid and he tries so hard. Why can't anyone help him?*

Chris took Xanthe four-wheeling today. They left about 9am, both in good spirits. At 1pm, Chris came bursting into the house by himself. I asked what was wrong and he got mad. "What the hell do you think is wrong? The boy freaked out, of course. Crying and whining and begging for you. He even flipped his four-wheeler over because he couldn't see through his goddamn tears. I am NEVER taking him again!"

I could hardly stand there waiting for him to finish. I was in a hurry to get to the garage and find my little boy. As I opened the door I expected the worst, but he was just standing there looking like his best friend had died. I pulled him into my arms. He immediately went into his version of what happened. "I tried to pretend I was sick when I first started missing you, but I could tell dad did not believe me. Then things just got worse. I missed you so much I couldn't concentrate and I flipped my four-wheeler. Then I started crying. Dad was mad. I tried to apologize on the way home, but he wouldn't listen. I am sorry, Mom. I really tried. I don't know what is wrong with me."

I gushed all sorts of phrases meant to console him. I wanted him to know that it wasn't his fault and that we loved him. He just stared at me. He had lost hope. I promised I would help him figure it all out. He just shook his head. "It doesn't matter anymore Mom, I will never get better. Why does my life have to suck? Why does this have to happen to me?"

I started crying and couldn't stop. He started crying too. We sat like that in the garage, holding each other for what seemed like forever. Finally, we went inside. I settled Xanthe on the couch and then looked at Chris with murder in my eyes. Why couldn't he support Xanthe? Would it be so hard for him to be empathetic once in a while? Sometimes I hate him. Xanthe just wants his love.

After awhile, Chris went out to the garage and I followed him. I was mad. Before I could say anything, Chris started to defend himself. He said he was sorry. I yelled that he could be nicer to Xanthe. "Don't you love him?"

I started to cry. Chris held me. He wiped my tears and whispered in my ear, "I do love him, I just get frustrated. When he first got upset I did try to settle him down. I just don't know how to do it. I felt like an idiot. And I drove an hour and a half today to go ride and minutes into it I had to pack up and come home again. I am mad and frustrated at the situation, not at him. I just want it all to get better."

I felt horrible for a moment. It was so easy to forget that he was frustrated too. In a way, I was proud of him. He didn't yell at Xanthe or blame him, he even tried his best to help. He was just upset at the circumstances. I guess if I want to vent every once in awhile, then he should be able to also. One more thing we needed to learn as a family.

Eventually, I tore myself loose from Chris' embrace and headed inside. I needed to talk to Xanthe. I wanted to explain Chris' side to him. Little did I know, I was about to become the student instead of the teacher. I sat next to Xanthe and started in with my explanation. Halfway through he cut me off. "I know already, Mom," he said. "I was there. That is why this is so hard. Dad really was trying to help me. I just couldn't calm down. That is why I feel so bad. He wanted to help me, but I am too messed up to be helped. I let him down."

I started to cry and smothered him with hugs. "You are not too messed up," I cried. "You both tried hard today, but today just wasn't the day for it to all work out. It will come. I promise!"

He just stared at me with disbelief and hopelessness. I couldn't think of anything more to say. I just held him and prayed.

MONDAY AUGUST 19TH

~ Last night was horrible, but of course, I expected it to be. Tears, fears, begging, pain. I tried to sell my soul to the devil in exchange for a cure for my son, but nothing happened. I guess that only works on TV. He was very upset this morning, anxious, crying, depressed, tired. I gave in and kept him home from school. I planned to spend the day pointing out all the positives of attending school and building him up for tomorrow. Of course, I also had to call in sick to work. My boss just stated that she would have to call me back. I wonder how that will go?

By dinnertime, I was exhausted again and would have done anything to get out of cooking. I stood in the pantry looking at all the boxed foods. *What do crazy moms make for dinner?* I wondered. I reached, smiling, for the family size box of macaroni and cheese. If we ever make it out of this situation alive, I am convinced that my family will never eat macaroni and cheese again. To say that I make it often would be the understatement of the year. For some reason, macaroni and cheese, cheese and turkey sandwiches and grilled cheese have become my staple dinners. Just the other day the kids asked me why everything we had for dinner had to have cheese in it. I told them to watch out or I would start planning breakfast and lunch around cheese too. They just rolled their eyes and laughed at me.

Bedtime was rough again tonight. I gave him two Benadryl at 8pm to help him sleep, but he was still awake at midnight. At 1am he finally fell asleep next to me on the sofa.

TUESDAY AUGUST 20ᵀᴴ

~ Different day, same scenario. The fear in his eyes was unbelievable. It hurt my heart to look at him. I held him instead. At that point I would have promised him the world to take the hurt away. I said he could stay home instead. Good decision? Probably not, but if you saw what I saw, you would have had a tough time doing it differently.

My boss called later in the day. Since I had done such a great job for them, they wanted to work with me on this situation. They had an offer. If I could give them a definite date (preferably next Monday) that I could resume work full-time and if I could guarantee that I would not take off any more unplanned time for the next year, then I would not be let go. As much as I wanted to jump at that offer, I knew it was impossible. If my life were that predictable, I wouldn't be in the situation I was in now. I told her ok out of confusion and fear and then hung up. Moments later, I realized I would have to call back and turn down the offer. I just can not choose work over my family. I hope they understand.

After a dinner of, you guessed it, grilled cheese, I put in an after hours call to Xanthe's psychiatrist. I begged for something to help him with the anxiety. She promised to call something in. Of course, the pharmacy doesn't open until 9am. So, tomorrow at school he will be without the extra help.

As we sat together on the sofa, I explained that we needed to make a plan. He needed to go to school tomorrow. He nodded his head. He knew what he needed to do. I felt horrible for bringing it up. I felt like telling him to "just get over the fear and go" was like telling a crippled child to "just walk, everyone else is." We talked, we planned, we agreed. I promised not to leave him, even if they tried to make me. I said I would take him home with me if they made me leave. He believed me. He smiled. My heart melted.

Bedtime went a little better tonight. Xanthe was still extremely anxious, but he was also worn out from all the worry. After about an hour of reassurances, he fell asleep.

WEDNESDAY AUGUST 21ST

~ Xanthe got up much easier this morning. I thought we were actually going to make it through school today. He showered, got dressed and off we went. The counselor set me up in room 103. Xanthe saw that I was staying there and headed off to class. We had agreed that he would stay for at least 3 periods, but more if he could make it. I only saw him between 1st and 2nd period. He didn't stop by on his way to 3rd period. That was a great sign. I felt like standing on the desk and shouting "Hallelujah." Instead, I just smiled and said a huge prayer of thanks! My feelings of euphoria did not last long, though. In walked the Special Education teacher. She had a few things to tell me. One, since Xanthe's records had not been sent from his old school yet, they could not accommodate him as a Special Education student. That meant no help with his locker, no one to help him in class, and no one to calm him down in his safe place. She suggested I keep him home until the records arrived and an IEP could be set up. The next words were the kicker, though. She had spoken to her boss, and they would not allow me to sit in the school anymore. They were against it. Couldn't they see that is was working? What did these people think was more important? My son showing up for school and overcoming his fear or their stupid one size fits all rules. Why did it always have to be so hard? Xanthe came in after 3rd period; he was ready to go home. He had no idea of what had just transpired. He was proud of himself. I decided not to tell him yet.

We headed to the pharmacy. Of course, the medication had to be ordered. Did I really think anything would go right today? They said it would be in around one tomorrow. A lot of good that does me. A day at school with no help and no medication to numb the fears. What did this world want from him?

Once at home, Xanthe fell asleep on the sofa. It was extremely hard work for him to accomplish what he did today. I sat on the floor beside him and patted his leg. I stared at his relaxed, sleeping face. "Please God," I prayed, "help us."

I started to cry. What will I do tomorrow? And how will I explain this to Chris? He will be furious if he comes home early and Xanthe is sleeping on the couch. Chris is sometimes resentful of Xanthe and now it was worse since I had lost my job. Chris blamed Xanthe, and Xanthe continued to try to win his love. It's a horrible circle that I would not wish upon my worst enemy. I dried my tears and got ready to leave for the elementary school. Life goes on and I had a daughter to pick up!

I called my boss right before five o'clock. I explained my decision to her. She said she understood and then gave me the number to human resources. I then called them. I was informed that I was "let go" as of today. We scheduled a time for me to come in and clean out my desk. After I hung up, I logged on to the Internet and applied for unemployment. I would have cried, but a part of me was relieved. Now there was one less thing in my life I had to stress out about. One less person I could let down.

Chris came home early and was in a good mood. I could see that he had worked through some of his frustration. I knew this had to be hell on him too. I made a special dessert to show him I appreciated his effort. And just to throw everyone off, I made a roast and potatoes for dinner. As I served it I exclaimed, "Look, no cheese!" That started everyone laughing.

The evening went well until bedtime. Xanthe was scared again… of school. I made a quick executive decision. I told him that he could stay home tomorrow. I figured that it was a good decision since he did not have an IEP or any medication to help. It didn't hurt that the school had suggested it. Before I fell into a restless sleep, I decided that I was going to go in to the school tomorrow to pour my heart out and hopefully get some help.

THURSDAY AUGUST 22ND

~ I dropped my daughter off at the elementary school at 7:50am and then headed to the middle school. My stomach was in knots. I had played out what I was going to say numerous times in my head. I sat in the parking lot for at least 15 minutes trying to get my confidence up to go inside.

I asked at the office for the counselor. She had called in sick today! I then asked for the Special Education teacher. They paged her to come down. When she arrived I asked if we could talk in private. Once at her room, she started in with talk about the IEP. I interrupted. My practiced words blurted out in a rush, "Before we talk about that, I need to get something off my chest. Ever since I left yesterday I have been confused and near tears. I try to do what the school wants me to do, while doing what I have to do for Xanthe. I feel as though I am failing. Everyone here keeps telling me different things, and I just want to do what is right. I want Xanthe in school just as much as you guys do, but we need help. Please, help us!"

This seemed to work. I could see her eyes soften as she stared at me. She explained to me that she was annoyed yesterday about how this situation was being handled. It seems that she and the social worker do not see eye to eye on this. We talked for over an hour. She was great. We set up a plan. She asked a lot of questions and gave me a few numbers to call for help. One of the numbers she gave me was for a full psychiatric evaluation at the area teaching hospital. I was impressed with the idea. We had never had that kind of testing done. All things considered, we decided to keep Xanthe out of school until Monday, when a plan would be in place. I breathed a sigh of relief. Could we be moving in the right direction?

I came home to find Xanthe still asleep. I thought about waking him, but decided instead to let him sleep in. He looked so peaceful, plus I needed the time to get my head together.

First, I got on the phone and called the insurance coordinator about the psychiatric evaluation. She was great this time. She was very concerned and sorry that Xanthe wasn't getting any better. She gave me the number to two hospitals that were covered under our insurance. Neither of them was the one the teacher had given me. I called both. The soonest anyone could see Xanthe was in November. On a whim, I called the non-covered hospital. They could get him in a week from Friday. I almost jumped for joy. I talked to the nurse for at least an hour. I asked a ton of questions. She was very knowledgeable, very patient and nice. Even though I would have to pay for the visit "out of pocket," I made the appointment. Here is what I have learned... The doctor-in-training starts from the beginning and asks questions about everything. They do not start with the present diagnosis because they do not want to be misled. The whole thing takes 2 or more hours. Then the doctor discusses his findings with highly trained doctors specializing in adolescent psychiatric issues. These doctors know about and understand the multitude of diseases and illness that could be causing the child's symptoms. They look for a diagnosis and any co-morbid conditions. Hopefully, this will be the answer we have been searching for!

We had a really good evening together. Everyone was in good spirits. I had filled Xanthe's new prescription earlier and he had taken it. I kept my eye on him all night for any side effects. As bedtime approached, I mistakenly believed that tonight was going to be easier. We had a good evening, and Xanthe knew he was not going to school tomorrow so there wasn't anything to be anxious about right? Wrong. Around eleven o'clock the mood roller coaster came crashing down. Xanthe woke me up because he was very upset. We went into the living room to talk. His words came out a mile a minute. "My life sucks, no one loves me, everything bad happens because of me, your life sucks because of me, nothing ever goes right, why do we even try..." and on and on like this for hours.

I tried to remember that this was the illness talking, but it still hurt. I took some of the things he said to heart. I had tried to give him a good life, but it felt as though I was failing. After awhile he screamed, "Why do I feel this way. I am so confused. I hate this!"

I wanted to cry. Instead, I asked him if he wanted to watch infomercials with me. This had become our middle of the night "thing." He smiled a very small smile of agreement. We cuddled on the couch, made fun of the programs and eventually, he fell asleep. I lay awake in the dark for hours, rubbing my son's back, wondering how we were ever going to make it through all of this.

FRIDAY AUGUST 23RD

~ Xanthe woke up in great spirits, ready to take on the world. I was exhausted. Tahni woke up and didn't want to go to school. She was tired too. I said she could stay home. I knew this was hard on her also. Maybe we all just needed a break!

The day went fairly well. Xanthe was very hyper. Running a mile a minute. He is hard to keep up with when he gets like this. He decided he was going to jump this big hill on our land with his 4-wheeler. This is a hill he has never jumped before. He has always been too scared to try it. Today, nothing could stop him from doing it. He had no fear. I stood outside and watched. Half of me wanted to watch incase he got hurt and the other half wanted to close my eyes until it was over. As he approached the jump, I almost shouted out, "Stop!" but I didn't and thankfully he made it. I was proud, but he was prouder. Of course, he wanted to do it again and again. I set a limit of three more times, and he seemed ok with that.

Later, I had to get dressed and go in to work to clean out my desk. My stomach was in knots for the entire drive. I waited in the lobby for my boss to come get me. We walked to my desk together. Everyone was looking at me, a few stopped to talk. Everyone was so sorry. They all understood. They wished me luck and said that they would keep me in their prayers. I threw my stuff in a box and got the hell out of there as fast as I could.

On the drive back home, I was out of it. For obvious reasons, I felt sad. I had worked hard to get where I was in the pharmaceutical research field. And I was good at what I did. A part of me was mourning for the achievements I would never reach. A part of me was going to miss doing something I enjoyed and excelled at. I was sad that part of my life was over for now.

Later today, we drove into town. Xanthe was going to his dad's for the weekend. They were going to a rock concert. Xanthe loves music, so I thought he would be all right. If not, his dad knew to call me and I would come get him. Tahni was staying with my mom for the weekend. They planned on driving to a shrine to light candles for all of us and pray for a miracle. Yesterday, as my sister and I made out the list of who needed the candles, we realized that a lot of people needed some help. Making the list helped me put my life in perspective. Even with our family troubles and the loss of my job, I have a lot to be thankful for.

Around five o'clock, I got a horrible phone call. My mom informed me that the middle school had been trying to get a hold of me all day. The message was…Do not bring Xanthe back to school on Monday. I panicked. Can a school refuse a child? What were my options now? What were we going to do? About 2 hours, numerous phone calls, and what felt like a heart attack later, I found out that the message was meant to say "just Monday" and that the principal had sounded apologetic as he explained that they just needed an extra day to set up all the services my son would need. When I heard all this, my body literally shook with relief.

By the time I fell into bed, I was a wreck. Today had been emotionally draining. Xanthe's hyper mood was hard to control. Tahni missing school had me worried. The loss of my job, and what I was supposed to do next, was weighing heavily on my mind. My problems with Chris were becoming overwhelming. And to top it all off, today would have been my dad's 68th birthday. I was feeling extra sad about not having him around since I had lost his ring. My head hurt with the burden of all these worries.

SUNDAY AUGUST 25TH

~ Yesterday was bad. I woke up early, even though I had planned to sleep in. Since both kids were gone, I wanted to catch up on my sleep, but my mind was too busy thinking bad thoughts. I should have gotten right up to get a head start on the day, but I couldn't get motivated. I had a list a mile long of things to do, but I either do not know how to do them, or I just didn't feel like doing them. I lay there for hours thinking about our lives. *Would it ever be possible to live like "normal" families? Would we all make it through this intact?*

When was it going to end?

Finally, my growling stomach made me get out of bed. I made myself some breakfast (a pop!) and puttered around the house. I could not relax. I felt anxious. It was weird without the kids around. Finally, I made a list of the things I needed to do, hoping that it would give me some sense of direction. It didn't. I wasted the entire day sitting on the sofa and reflecting on our lives.

Today I was more energetic. I hopped out of bed, showered and then did some much needed housework. I needed to head into town around 11 am to pick up the kids. I ran around getting things done and the time flew by.

Tahni was waiting for me as I pulled into my mom's driveway. She ran up and gave me a big hug. I spent the next hour listening to the details of her trip and receiving my presents from the shrine. Tahni looked happy and that made me smile. I interrupted her story long enough to call their dad. He and Xanthe had just woken up. Since we had awhile until Xanthe was ready, Mom, Tahni and I decided to go out for Chinese food. Tahni was very hyper. She was laughing, talking loudly and being silly. We all had a great time. It was fun to think about nothing but eating and laughing for a few hours.

When we got back to the house Tahni called her friend that lived down the street and then went there to play for an hour. That gave mom and me some time to ourselves. We played a computer game and then just sat and talked. She is so strong. She is my rock. I told her I was worried about both Xanthe and Tahni. Xanthe is not getting any better and Tahni is worrying me. Tahni has become very clingy and she doesn't want to go to school. She is also reduced to tears way too easily. I thought that maybe she needed someone to talk to. I also told mom about the evaluation I had scheduled. She was hopeful that it would work. I felt better after talking to her. She always finds a way to make me see the silver lining.

Finally, about 6pm I left and picked up the kids. The drive home was good. We talked about our weekends and got caught up. Xanthe had a great time at the concert. He seemed a little tired and irritable, but all in all, he seemed ok.

The evening went well. Chris came home late. He had to work 13 hours today. We ate dinner; we talked. Everyone was in good spirits. After dinner we settled down to watch some TV. We were in what Xanthe calls "chair mode." We stayed that way until bedtime.

Chris went on to bed and I headed off to put the dogs up for the night. Xanthe followed me. I knew something was up when he did that. Anytime things are not right with him, he needs to be close to me. I asked him what was bothering him. He said he was scared and his stomach hurt. Tahni and I decided to pray using our new shrine stuff. All three of us piled on the sofa. Xanthe watched TV while Tahni and I prayed. Not even half way through our prayers, Xanthe fell asleep next to me. Tahni and I finished up and then I lead Xanthe to bed.

I laid awake in the dark and said some extra prayers of thanks. I was relieved. It seemed as though Xanthe would be sleeping normally tonight. I whispered "thank you" one last time and closed my eyes with a smile on my face.

MONDAY AUGUST 26ᵀᴴ

~ I am finding it hard to convey the emotion of the last twelve hours in words. Shortly after I fell asleep last night, Xanthe woke me up. He was scared. We went to sit in the living room together. That is when he lost it. He started crying, sobbing actually. His whole body shook with the tears. For the next 3 hours he went on and on about how scared he was. He was completely convinced that something bad was going to happen. Every little sound made him jump; every noise brought fresh fear to his face. I tried to hold him, to console him but nothing I did or said seemed to work. He even made me stand in the bathroom with him as he went. He was afraid that if he left my sight, even for a minute, someone would take him. This was the first time I was unable to eventually calm him down.

He was convinced that he heard someone using a glasscutter to break in through the windows. I tried to explain away the sounds. He heard other noises too. Someone walking, someone breathing, someone opening the door. Xanthe was very jumpy. Panic caused his eyes to dart around the room. His body shivered in fear. Finally, around 4am Xanthe fell asleep in my arms. Not because he was finally relaxed, but because exhaustion had taken over. I took him into bed and held him the rest of the night.

Of course, at 6:30am the alarm went off. I had to get up to take Tahni to school. My eyes were so heavy, I could barely hold them open. Tahni woke up in a very bad mood. She couldn't find a shirt she liked, then she had no pants to wear. Then her hair wouldn't come out right. Finally, she broke down into tears. I went to hold her. She pushed me away. I let her vent. "No one understands me, Mom," she screamed. "Everyone is always saying poor Xanthe; he is bipolar. Well, what about me? No one even cares about me anymore. If I am talking and Xanthe interrupts, everyone listens to him. Everyone lets him pick everything so that he is not sad. Everything revolves around him. I hate it!"

Then she collapsed into more tears. I held her and I apologized. We talked. I promised to do better. She promised to talk things out before they exploded again. We checked the clock. 8:20. Now, Tahni was late for school. She started crying again. "Mom," she pleaded. "I can't go like this. My eyes are red, I am still crying and my teacher is mean if you are late."

I knew we could pull it together and she could go, but I gave in. *Was it because I was so tired, because she was so upset or even because we were both so stressed out?* I do not know. I only know that at the time my heart couldn't take making her go to school. Maybe I needed to be near her, to know that she knew I cared. We cuddled on the sofa and she fell asleep.

Around nine noises from the bedroom startled me out of a restless sleep. Xanthe was up. I instantly dreaded his entrance into the living room. What kind of mood would he be in today? Thankfully it was a good one.

We actually had a relatively calm day today. It was one of those rare days were Xanthe seemed almost normal. No major mood shifts, no sadness or mania. I should have felt relaxed, but I didn't. I held my breath all day waiting for a break down. By bedtime, I was completely drained. Thankfully, the kids were too. By 10pm we were all in bed and quickly drifting off to sleep.

TUESDAY AUGUST 27TH

~ Tahni went to school without a fight today and Xanthe stayed home because his IEP meeting was not until 2pm today and the school didn't want him back until tomorrow. So far so good.

I spent the day preparing for the IEP meeting. I wrote down the good points about school so far, Xanthe's strengths and weaknesses, and the accommodations I thought we would need. I also gathered his old report cards, test scores and a small handout on Childhood On-set Bipolar Disorder. I was scared, but hopeful.

I arrived at the school a little early, but I had some time to wait. They were not quite ready for me and we ended up starting the meeting twenty minutes late. Once we started, everything went pretty well. They had a plan set up to get Xanthe back into school, slowly. They had drawn it up in contract form for Xanthe and me to sign. It stated, in fancy terms, that he would attend school tomorrow for one period, then stay for two periods the next day and so on until he was present for an entire day. They also agreed to let me stay in room 103 throughout this transition period. They had informed all of his teachers about his condition and designated a safe place for him to go when he lost control. They had done a very thorough and understanding job. I left the meeting feeling very good about tomorrow and the school year in general.

Once at home, I explained the contract and it's conditions to Xanthe. He seemed to be comfortable with the plan. Since he had stayed for 3 periods before, he was pretty confident that he could make it through one tomorrow. I didn't know what to think. What Xanthe wanted to do and what he ended up being able to do, were two totally different things. If he couldn't even go four-wheeling with family, how was he supposed to go to school with strangers? I didn't express my concerns though. Better that he think I was totally convinced of his success.

Considering all that went on today, bedtime was easy. Xanthe was still psyched about the plan, Tahni was feeling better and Chris was in a good mood. With all of my ducks in a row for the moment, I took advantage of the situation and shooed everyone into bed. If only it was always this easy.

WEDNESDAY AUGUST 28ᵀᴴ

~ What a horribly rotten day! I do not know how much more of this we can take. I am about ready to quit trying and just stay at home every day with my kids and ignore the rest of the world!

The morning started out well enough. Xanthe had slept all night. Both he and Tahni got ready for school without a fight. We went over the plan for the day and he agreed with it all. He was going to stay all day, I was going to stay in room 103 all day, and we were going to go fishing after school to celebrate. I knew he only had to make it for an hour, but he was psyched to do an entire day and I didn't want to fight it.

As we walked into the school, he was laughing and doing great. The social worker met us at the door and walked me to room 103 as Xanthe took off for his locker. Within minutes, he came bursting into room 103 upset. He couldn't get his locker open. When he turned to ask for help, he was overcome by hordes of kids fighting their way down the hall to get to class. He immediately fell apart. In his panic, he lost direction and couldn't find room 103. By the time he found me, he was completely overcome with fear. He started crying and begging to go home. I took a deep breath. I knew I needed to calm him down before I could reason with him enough to get him to stay at school. I mentally ran through the few techniques I had learned, but before I settled on one, the social worker stepped in. She started asking him questions. "What happened? Why can't you go to class? What are you afraid of? Are you even trying to calm down? Are you listening to me?"

When he wouldn't respond, she changed tactics. She tried to lay down the rules. "It's the law that you go to school. All the other kids have to go. You need to calm down." At first he just kept saying, "I don't know, I don't know." Then he freaked out, got mad and told her to leave him alone.

She replied, "Don't get snippy with me." At that comment, Xanthe ran to the corner, hid behind a file cabinet and cried. I tried to talk to her first. I tried to explain that this is what bipolar kids do when they feel overwhelmed. She didn't buy it. She wanted me to make him calm down so that she could talk to him. I tried to explain how I was trying to do that. I explained that I needed to calm him down first, before I broached the subject of going to class. I explained my plan and justified it with a comment about learning it from our mental health professionals and books.

She met all this with, "Are you saying I am not a professional?" I said, "No, I am saying that everyone has opinions on how to handle this and I have to pick one and stick with it. If I listen to all of the differing opinions out there then there would be no consistency so I choose to listen to his psychiatrist."

She then informed me that he was just throwing a temper tantrum and acting like a spoiled child. I almost started to cry. I ask her what she wanted me to do then, and she said, "Get over there and calm him down." I asked how? She stated again, "Just get over there and calm him down."

I went over and sat beside Xanthe. He wouldn't let me touch him. First, I tried to slow his breathing with the relaxation techniques we had learned. Then I brought up things to visualize. Finally, I had him start naming 80's hair bands. The social worker sat there staring at us, rubbing her temples like she was annoyed, fed up with the whole situation and wasting her time. It made me uncomfortable. I suddenly felt like an idiot, sitting behind a file cabinet with my son, naming rock bands. I started doubting myself. This doubt must have come through in my voice or my actions, because Xanthe immediately became upset again. When he started to cry again, the social worker got up and left. She didn't say a word to me, so I had no idea what she up to.

Within minutes the room began to fill. The principal, the school physiologist, the special education teacher, even a paraprofessional, had come to witness our pain. I was upset at first, but managed not to show it. The principal began his questions first. He was very calm and understanding as I explained the situation to him. In the end, they all were great. They spoke to him in a calm direct manner and didn't push him too far when he started to fall apart. They all understood what had happened and they supported my plan to calm him down first and get him into class second. After Xanthe told the story of his morning, it was decided that we would take the lock off of his locker, he would stay until the end of fourth period today, I could stay with him, and we would both sit in room 103 and do make-up work. I really appreciated all of their understanding and support. I felt good about the plan. After they all left, I easily calmed Xanthe down and we spent three hours doing English and math make-up work.

Before we left for the day, I stopped in at the office to turn in the finished work and to talk to the social worker. I wanted to confront her about this morning. I asked her if I had done something to get on her bad side. I explained that I felt very upset after our earlier conversation. I explained that I never meant to insinuate that she was not a professional and that I felt she was attacking my parenting skills. She acted very defensive and was hard to talk to. She even denied saying Xanthe was spoiled. I replied, "Well, I clearly heard you say it."

She responded with, "I would never say that. I don't know what you think you heard, but I never said that."

I tried to argue the point, but she was insistent that it never happened. It was unreal. She then accused me of dragging my feet on getting her the information she needed to service Xanthe. I explained that the school personnel kept changing their minds on exactly what they wanted, but that I had given them everything that they had requested so far. She dismissed that with, "Well, I do not want to beat the point here, all I am saying is that we need to work together, and you need to go back to his medical team, explain strongly what is going on with Xanthe, and get some answers."

I just turned and left at that point feeling exhausted, defeated and hopeless. I walked out to the office to get Xanthe. He was talking with the paraprofessional. That guy is awesome with Xanthe. He tried to talk to me too, but I could feel the tears welling up in my eyes. I managed to thank him without losing control, he wished us luck and we left.

I stayed strong on the drive home and pretended to be happy for Xanthe's sake. He was feeling bad though. He apologized for making the morning so bad. He said he was sorry for putting me through all of this. I told him it was all right and that I didn't mind. I tried to reassure him and let him know that it wasn't him or anything that he was doing that was upsetting me, it was other people and their ignorance. He asked for a hug. Of course, I obliged.

Shortly after we arrived home, Xanthe fell asleep on the couch. I wanted to write everything down before I forgot it, but I was mentally tired. I lay down with Xanthe for about an hour instead. As I lay there, the events of the morning kept running through my mind. As it usually goes, I thought of a million different ways that I could have controlled the situation differently. One thing really stuck in my mind. When the social worker accused me of questioning her professionalism I wish I had said, *Your PROFESSIONAL job is to help people in crisis, correct? Well, I am in crisis and from what I have seen, I have to question your ability to handle that!*

Later, I picked Tahni up from school and found out that she had had a bad day also. I listened and tried to console her. I figured that there was more going on here than just a strict teacher. I have been in denial for awhile, but I am really beginning to see the effects of this illness on my daughter. I think it is time to get her in to see someone. She needs someone to vent her feelings to.

The evening went about the same as every other evening. Xanthe was nervous, irritable and physically ill from worrying about tomorrow. Knowing that the evaluation was only two days away, I said he could stay home from school. If everyone was working together and if we weren't causing him more stress with all the changes and bickering, I would have made him go. But with the way things were, I was convinced it would be better to wait until we had something concrete to go on.

Even with the knowledge that he was staying home tomorrow, Xanthe was still very upset at bedtime. I cheated and gave him two Benadryl to make him sleep. He dozed off about an hour later. He only woke me up four times all night, and each time he was fairly easy to console and calm down.

THURSDAY AUGUST 29™

~ Another bad morning, another bad decision on my part. The alarm went off at 7am and I went to wake Tahni. She immediately became upset. Crying, saying she was tired, her teacher was mean and so on. At that very moment, my mind finally snapped. I just didn't have it in me any longer to keep up the fight. All at once I felt very small, very useless and very scared. Even with all my effort, I had failed. I now had two very messed up kids, both of which couldn't (or wouldn't?) go to school. I decided we all needed more help than we were getting. I ran to the kitchen and called the insurance coordinator. It was too early for her to be in, so I left a message. I called both kids in sick to school, then I sat down and cried. Today, I decided, I am going to find someone we can all talk to, someone who understands this illness and hopefully, someone who can see us today. Our lives are falling apart. I will beg, if I have to. I know we have the evaluation appointment tomorrow, but I need help now!

I called the insurance coordinator again, because I was tired of waiting for her to return my call. I was antsy for some action. I told her what was going on. She must have heard the desperation in my voice. She felt bad for me and promised to find us some help. I huddled on the sofa with the kids while we waited for her to call us back.

As they watched TV, my mind reeled with all the things that needed to be done. I needed to find a job, I needed to help my son and

I definitely needed to get some help for my daughter. I also needed to find a way to get them both back into school. I started to feel overwhelmed as even the mundane stuff started to filter into my mind. I needed a shower. I needed to do the dishes. I needed to buy food for dinner. I needed to clean the house. I needed to breathe.

I jumped up in frustration and announced that we were going to the library. I have always found comfort in books, but lately I have been too depressed and anxious to read. I was convinced though that there had to be a book out there that could help me pull our lives together a little better until we could get some professional help. The kids love the library too, so this idea was not too hard to pull off.

After hours at the library, I came home with four books about bipolar disorder. I immediately started reading. I finished the first one in two hours. It didn't really help much though. The kid in the book was suffering from different things than my son was, and there were no real details as to what the family did to keep their lives together on a day to day basis. I was slightly disappointed, but still hopeful. I still had 3 books left to read!

Just before five, I heard back from the insurance coordinator. She had found a doctor for us. She seemed to think he was a perfect match. I wrote down the name and number and vowed to call him tomorrow.

FRIDAY AUGUST 30TH

~ The sun worked its way past my heavy eyelids and my brain realized it was morning. I sat up excited. Today was the day. I called both kids in sick to school, made us a quick breakfast and we hit the road. In hindsight I should have known that I was putting too much hope into this one appointment, but at the time I truly believed that this was to be our answer.

Xanthe, Tahni, their dad and I arrived early for the appointment. They sat down in the waiting room while I filled out all the usual paperwork. The doctor was running behind, of course, so we were finally called back thirty minutes late. The doctor lead us to her small office and the questions began. They were mostly questions we had heard a million times before, and had answered a million times before. I described exactly what our days and nights were like. She asked about medications, school attendance, my pregnancy with him, our family history and his social interactions. Finally, she started asking him questions. After what seemed like hours she led us all to the waiting room so that she could discuss her findings with the chief doctor.

While we waited, I began to feel let down. Somehow I knew that we were not going to be leaving here with our "miracle cure." I expressed this concern to Xanthe's dad. He just told me not to give up hope. I sat and thought, lost in my fears, while the three of them laughed and talked.

Finally, the chief doctor strolled into the room. He seemed nice, intelligent and concerned. What the entire conversation boiled down to was three main points. One, he felt that Xanthe was on too many medications, two of which could cause problems if taken together. He discontinued the Propolonal and the Adderall, but he added a medication strictly for anxiety, Celexa. Two, he felt that the bipolar diagnosis might not be the only thing going on in this case and third, we would need to come back for more testing for them to be sure. I wanted to scream or cry or throw something. Instead, I shook both doctors' hands, accepted the new prescription and literature and quietly made my way to the car. The kids were going home with their dad for the night and I was headed home.

As I drove home, I let my mind wonder. All I could think about was writing down today's events, taking a long bath and then going to sleep. I didn't have the strength to face the doctor's words. More waiting, more trying, no cure. I also longed for someone to confide in. Someone to take the weight of the world off my shoulders for an hour or two. Or even just someone to hold me and help me feel less alone.

I tried to go to sleep since my body was exhausted, but my mind would not cooperate. I tried to write as I lay awake in the living room, but I was stuck. I had so many things going on in my mind, but I could not put them all together. I felt numb. Today had saddened me in a way I hadn't been saddened in a long time. I felt hopeless. Now, I had doubts that Xanthe was even bipolar. On one hand, this could be a good thing because it would explain why nothing has worked to help him so far. On the other hand, it could mean that we were back to square one. My son has a problem, yet we do not know what it is, so we do not know how to treat it. And if it turns out to be a different illness, will we have to go through months or years of trying first one thing and then another until we find the right treatment again? Can Xanthe make it through all that? Can I? Can his sister and his dad and Chris?

Eventually I forced myself to get up and call the new doctor. I was immediately disappointed. He sounded very old and he was against the diagnosis of bipolar in children. It took everything I had not to cry. I answered all of his questions and quietly retold our history. We made an appointment for Thursday. I hung up with every intention of canceling the appointment the next day. I just didn't feel good about this doctor.

SATURDAY AUGUST 31ST

~ I woke up late today and lay in bed for hours. There didn't seem to be any reason to move. I was too tired to even cry. I tried to shut my eyes and go back to sleep, but too many thoughts kept running through my mind.

Still in my pajamas and out of it mentally, I drove into to town around noon to pick Tahni up. Xanthe was staying at his dad's one more night so that they could go fishing. Tahni hates fishing, so she opted to come home with me. After picking her up, we went to my mom's. Mom tried to engage me in conversation, but I was quiet. All day I felt numb to the world. Tahni was in a terrible mood, which was worsened by the fact that I was unresponsive. In desperation for attention, she asked if she could have a friend spend the night. Of course, I said yes. This would give her something to keep her happy and occupied and leave me free to wallow in my self-pity.

Still too tired to make any real effort at life, I stopped off for a pizza for dinner and a box of doughnuts and a gallon of milk for breakfast. It wasn't the most nutritious fare, but at least they wouldn't starve to death.

The night went smoothly enough. Tahni and her friend played numerous games and then built a tent out of blankets and slept under it in the living room. I wasted the night staring at the TV and hoping for sleep. A few times I found the energy to smile or laugh for the sake of the girls, but mostly I just stayed locked in my self-pity. At ten, I left the girls and went to bed knowing full well that sleep would not come easily.

SUNDAY SEPTEMBER 1ST

~ We all slept late and then Tahni and her friend played until it was time to take her home. They were having a blast. I could see that it had been good for Tahni to play with someone who didn't suffer from mood swings or extreme irritability or extreme laziness (me!). I was feeling better and more energetic, so I decided to clean the house.

Around three, we headed into to town to take her friend home and pick up Xanthe. When we got to their dad's to pick up Xanthe, he informed me of the terrible night that Xanthe had had. I was hoping that the new medication was making things better, but it appeared that the severe anxiety was still very much present. Thankfully, Xanthe was in a good mood today, even though he was tired.

Once back in town, the three of us went to the grocery store. We had a blast. We were laughing and talking and being silly as we searched the aisles for something to eat that didn't contain cheese. It was nice. I have learned to appreciate these little moments over the years. An hour and a half later, we were running through the rain with our bags and loading the car as quickly as we could. We were all smiles and drenching wet.

Dinner went well, but then Xanthe started to turn moody and acted bored. In desperation to save his good mood, I suggested that he and Tahni write songs together. They do this sometimes when they are getting along. They both have aspirations of being in a band.

Later they came into the living room, bored again. Chris and I entertained them by playing a video game. The kids laugh when Chris and I play against each other because I usually win and Chris is a funny loser. He makes up crazy excuses like the sun was in his eyes or his hand had a spasm. I had dosed Xanthe with his nighttime medications and two Benadryl before we started playing. About an hour later, Xanthe was out. So he was easy to get to bed. He only woke me once to say he was scared and I was able to calm him down fairly quickly.

MONDAY SEPTEMBER 2ND

~ I woke up first this morning. We were having my mom, sister and nieces out for a barbecue. I had a few things I needed to start cooking. Tahni was up next. She helped me in the kitchen and then watched TV. My mom came out around eleven o'clock. Xanthe was still asleep and Chris was mad about it. He made some comment about waking him up so that he wouldn't keep us up all night. I just shrugged it off. I knew Chris was in a bad mood because of money worries and I also knew that no matter what time Xanthe got up, he would either sleep tonight or he wouldn't. Xanthe got up on his own though about thirty minutes later. I had him go start the grill. He loves that job. He is convinced he is a grill king.

Mom called Roger while she was at our house. I asked to talk to him when she was done. He knew how upset I had been lately, since I had called him a few times since that Sunday that he had helped me so much. Today though, I was going to ask for more than a sympathetic ear. Since I had lost my job, Chris has been trying to pick up as many hours as possible, but the loss of my income was going to hurt us. On top of that, we had to pay for the evaluation with our own money, and we had to pay the co-pay on yet another prescription. To make matters worse, I had been denied unemployment until my appeal meeting scheduled for a week from Wednesday. Money was tight and it was just getting tighter. Chris and I were panicked as to how we were going to make our mortgage payment. I swallowed my pride and asked Roger for some money. He was very understanding about it and said he would have been mad if I hadn't asked for it. I promised to pay him back and I meant it, I just didn't know when it would be!

Dinner and the rest of the afternoon went well. After my family left, Xanthe and Tahni started getting bored. Xanthe went out to ride his 4-wheeler and Tahni took a bath. When they both came back into the living room, they were in better moods again. We spent the rest of the evening watching TV and cuddling on the sofa.

As the evening wore on, I tried not to think about what tomorrow held. Xanthe's dad and I were going to the middle school to meet with everyone. We wanted to make a new plan, inform them of how the evaluation went and try to clear the air between the social worker and us. We had agreed to let both Xanthe and Tahni stay home from school, yet again. Xanthe, because we wanted to get things settled for him before we made him go back and Tahni, because she had forgotten to bring her make-up work home the other day, so I was going to get her books for her and let her get caught up. She was still feeling upset about her teacher and she was still having a hard time with her feelings, so we wanted to try to make it as easy on her as possible. We did stress to both of them though that this was the last time, for awhile, that they could stay home and that they both HAD to go to school on Wednesday! To the outside world this probably sounds like a very bad idea, but when you are living in a constant state of anxiety, confusion and stress you do weird things, and more importantly, weird things are sometimes necessary.

Bedtime went well for Xanthe and Tahni, but I couldn't shut my mind off long enough to go to sleep. My life felt like it was spinning out of control. No matter what I tried most days, I couldn't calm Xanthe or Tahni. In fact, there wasn't much each day I could control.

TUESDAY SEPTEMBER 3RD

~ Today went better than I could have imagined at the school. Xanthe's dad drove out for the meeting. The social worker couldn't be there, but the rest of the team was. We told them about the mixed results of the evaluation. They acted very understanding and sympathetic. We switched a lot of classes for Xanthe. Now, instead of going to the regular seventh grade math and language arts classes, he would be going to learning center. That would relieve some of his stress and hopefully make it possible for him to learn. He is very behind in both of these areas. Last time he was tested, he was reading at a fourth grade level. The discouraging part about it is that his IQ test shows him to be borderline genius. All the time he has missed and his inability to concentrate during the rough times, has caused him to be unable to learn.

We also discussed having the special education teacher re-test him to find out exactly where he is academically. This will be a big help in getting him the information he needs to get caught up.

We didn't get to clear the air with the social worker since she wasn't there, but we did arrange for Xanthe not to have to see her if he didn't want too. His new "safe place" is with the special education teacher.

I drove home feeling better than I had in awhile. With all of these accommodations in place and the fact that the school staff was being so understanding, I truly believed we could get Xanthe back into school.

I did receive some great news today. I think I might have found a job. I will be processing medical claims for doctors. It is still in the medical field, so that makes me feel better and I will be able to do the job from home. I just need to brush up on my coding skills and get the software to do the job. That of course, is the one down fall to the job. I obviously do not have the cash lying around to spend. I have faith though, that it will work out if it is meant to be.

The evening and then bedtime went fairly well. Xanthe was

nervous, but determined to make it tomorrow and I had dosed him with Benadryl again so that helped him fall asleep.

As usual, I plan on praying once I get in bed. I plan to pray for help for Xanthe in making it through the school day. I have to admit that until recently, praying is not something that I did everyday or even every week. I was raised Catholic, but I was never very serious about it. I was more of the thinking that, as long as I was living my life in the best and kindest way possible, I was showing my love for a greater power. My prayers consisted of things like thank you for the great day, or my new job, or my wonderful life or even for a green light when I was in a hurry to get to Xanthe. And sometimes I prayed for help when the people I loved were sick or sad or having a rough time. But now I pray every day, sometimes more than once, in hopes that someone will make things easier for my son. I never pray for a cure, because I believe that there are other children out there with fatal diseases that need a cure. We just need help in dealing with the symptoms. My son will live, but I want him to live happy.

WEDNESDAY SEPTEMBER 4TH

~ This morning started out easily enough. Xanthe was nervous, but I managed to calm him down enough to go to class. I went to room 103 as usual, and he took off for his locker. I held my breath until the bell rang, hoping that he would make it into his first class. He made it through that one, but then he broke down before the second one. He came flying into room 103 all tears and panic. Right or wrong we left. On the ride home I explained that I was proud of him, but that he needed to make it through more classes tomorrow. We agreed on three hours. He was shaking and tired, but I think also proud and relieved.

I called the new psychologist with every intention of canceling our appointment. I still couldn't bring myself to believe he could help, my impression of him led me to believe he would just be like every one else. All talk and no cure. When he answered something changed my mind. I don't know if I truly believe in divine intervention, but someone or something was telling me to keep the appointment. I made up a quick excuse, claimed to be calling to verify our appointment and hung up. My hands shook as I placed the phone in its cradle. I have no idea what actually happened, but the feeling that came over me was very strong. Odd.

So, I guess we are going to go, but I am not going to put as much hope into this visit as I did the last. At least by keeping the appointment, I am trying to get us some help. I do not know how much longer we can do this. Every second of every day I am waiting for Xanthe to freak out, and for Tahni to break down into tears. It has become my full time job to try and predict when a melt down might occur and then to do everything in my power to keep it from happening. I feel as though I haven't truly let down my guard in years.

Good news again today. Chris cleared more on his check than he anticipated, so I will be able to take the job. Now I just need to find the time to study all those codes!

Bedtime was horrible. Tahni was overly tired and cranky. Xanthe was anxious. I stayed up until 1am with him going over all of the possible outcomes for tomorrow. We covered everything from locker failure to earthquake drills before he finally fell asleep.

THURSDAY SEPTEMBER 5TH

~ This morning started out horribly. Both kids woke up complaining of stomach aches. The problem with that is I never know if these symptoms are real or pretend. And I never know if I am supposed to be sympathetic like other moms or forceful, because they are using these pains as an excuse to stay home. I decided to try the forceful path. As my daughter got out the car for school, she was in tears. I stood my ground, but on the inside I was crying. It broke my heart as I watched her, hunched over, walking into the school trying to stop her tears. Another time where I will have to question whether I did the right thing or not.

Life was just as bad when we arrived at the middle school. Xanthe was crying in the back seat. I was still playing the forceful role. I explained to him that even though his stomach hurt, he still had to get out of the car and go in. I even pointed out that I had just made his sister go to school even though she was crying and her stomach hurt. I went on to point out that sometimes you just have to do hard things. This was a lecture I had given him a million times. Sometimes I felt that this lecture was a great idea and other times I felt like I was asking him to heal himself so that life will be easier. Which is right? No one seems to know. Believe me, I have asked everyone.

We eventually made it into the school and Xanthe went to his first hour. He did come to me upset after that, but instead of saying we could go home I sat there and pretended to read a magazine and made him stay through third period. No, he wasn't in class, but I figured that at least he was in school. We would have had to leave then anyway since he had the appointment with the new psychologist. Xanthe was tired when we did leave and he slept the entire drive to the doctor's office.

The psychologist appointment went better than I had hoped. This guy seemed to understand that Xanthe couldn't help what he was feeling and doing because he had never been given the tools to change things. But he did stress to Xanthe that the only way he was going to get better was to help himself. He wasn't overly forceful or cruel with that advice though, so Xanthe didn't freak out. The biggest thing was that after we discussed all the problems we were having, the psychologist asked Xanthe what one thing he would like to solve first. Xanthe stated simply, "I want to quit missing my Mom so much so that I can go to school and have fun and stuff."

I almost cried. His request hit me hard. It made me realize that over the years, since I was the only one that stood by him and tried to understand, I had become the one place he felt the safest. If that never changed then he would never be able to leave me.

The psychologist did say a few things though, that left me feeling paranoid. He asked a bunch of questions about how I interact with Xanthe and other people. He thought it was odd that I feel sad when I see my dogs at the door wanting to come in. I usually let them in. He said something about me being in charge and not the dogs. He then told me to get a water gun and squirt them so they wouldn't sit at the door and beg. I told him that that was mean. All the dogs wanted was someone to play with. He looked at me like "Hmmm." I wonder what that meant and why we were talking about my dogs.

After the appointment I had a lot of time to think. I started second-guessing myself. Maybe I was holding Xanthe back. Maybe I was co-dependent. Maybe I did make it easier for him to be sick. All day I flipped back and forth from thinking that I was making him worse to thinking that I was just doing the best I could. I did not want him to rely on me so much. In fact, I was always trying to get his dad or Chris to take him for the weekend or even a few hours so that I could have some time by myself or with Tahni. I also wanted other people to see what he was going through. Maybe they could help more than I could. Part of the reason I do not want to home school him is because I want to have my own life. Of course, when I try to send him away for a few hours, I feel guilty, but I selfishly look forward to that time. I think I am going to call the psychologist tomorrow and tell him how I feel and see if he has any advice for me. The bottom line is that I want to help Xanthe have a normal life, and I will do whatever I have to do to achieve that. So if I am part of the problem, I am willing to accept that and change. I just need someone to tell me what I am doing wrong and what I need to be doing that is right. Again, I just need help.

Tahni's appointment wasn't until 5pm. I left Xanthe with Chris during the appointment. On the drive over I asked her if she wanted me to go in with her or not. I had already given the psychologist the background on Tahni and why we needed this visit. I wanted her to know that I would be there for her if she needed me to be, but I also wanted her to be able to talk about her true feelings without having to worry about my reaction. I was afraid that she had things to say about living with Xanthe in general and my reactions to it specifically. I wanted her to be free to talk about anything. In the end she chose to go in alone. I sat in the lobby for an hour and a half enjoying my short break and half nervous about what was bothering Tahni.

Ten minutes before the end of the session the doctor sent Tahni out and asked me in. He had nothing but good things to report. He stated that she was a well adjusted child, given the circumstances and that she was very mature for her age. He also set my mind at ease about the long term effects of all of this on her. He insisted that she was coping well. He liked the idea of our "Mommy/Tahni" days and told me to increase their occurrence. He also said that she was just feeling a little overwhelmed, but that she knew that she could come to me anytime. She was also very worried about her brother. All in all, she was just suffering from appropriate concerns, and her "off" days were just her way of venting and letting off steam. Some of it was also due to her age. Eleven is a rough age for girls. He told me to keep the lines of communication open and to keep trying to single her out for some one-on-one time. He wasn't concerned about her mental health, but he did want to see her at least one more time. *Not bad* I thought as I left his office, *Maybe I am actually doing something right!*

Bedtime was bad again. This time Xanthe was depressed. His complaints ranged from everyone thinking he was a loser since he was never at school, to his thinking that he would never be able to pull off an entire day there. He was being pretty hard on himself, and his self-esteem seemed to have bottomed out. Somehow I managed to quiet him down and he fell asleep shortly after midnight.

FRIDAY SEPTEMBER 6TH

~ Today went horribly, as well. Xanthe was upset the minute I woke him up. As the minutes ticked by, it just got worse. Finally, as he was throwing up in the bathroom and crying and begging to stay home, I gave up and called him in sick to school. The principal answered the phone and I felt like a failure as I told him that Xanthe wouldn't be in today. Whether it was imagined or real, I felt that the school staff was thinking that I was not trying hard enough. They had totally gone out of their way to afford him every accommodation they could. They had done everything short of going to class for him.

Now, all we had to do was get him into the building and for the last few days I had not been able to do even that. He is too big for me to pick up and drag to school. And if I did manage to do that, he would just cry and throw up there. I have no idea what the right thing to do in this situation is.

On a brighter note, Tahni went to school without a single problem. She even seemed excited to go, something to do with a cool day during band. Whatever the reason was, she was up and around early and anxious to get out the door.

My cousin came by to visit today. After I told her the story of our morning, she asked me why I didn't just home school him. I recited the same four reasons I kept repeating to anyone who asked. One, if I do not make him face this problem and fear, what do I do when the next one comes up? Do we just find a way to avoid that one too? Two, how will he ever make friends and have a life away from our house and me if he never leaves? He would miss out on so much. Three, I do not know how to teach kids, if I did I would have become a teacher. I know I could do it if I had to, but I am not very patient and I find it very hard to explain new things to people so that they can understand. And four, I selfishly want to have some time to purse my own life, my job and my dreams. If Xanthe wasn't ill I could do this and be with him at the same time, but when he is home I can not even shower without reassuring him, let alone hold down a job or finish an activity. Sometimes I think the fourth reason makes me a bad mom, other times I think that if the fourth reason makes me feel bad then that means that I am co-dependent. Help! I am so confused. My cousin left feeling just as confused as I was.

I had called the psychologist right after eight, but had to leave a message. When he finally called me back, I described this morning's events and asked him what I was supposed to be doing in situations like that. I felt really good after talking to him. For the first time ever, someone actually gave me some practical, tangible advice and told me that I was doing the right thing. He agreed that I could not pick Xanthe up and force him into school. He did suggest that I go out and get in the car. Since Xanthe doesn't want to be without me he will probably follow. Then I am to do the same thing at school. Get out of the car and go on in. Xanthe will presumably follow me in. Now, this does not answer how I am supposed to get him to go to class, but at least he will be at school and they won't be able to call social services on me for keeping my child at home. Funny law, I think. They only care that he is physically at the school. It doesn't matter if the entire time he is there he is crying and throwing up in the social worker's office.

The psychologist and I also talked about Xanthe's condition. The psychologist is still stumped. He does not believe in the bipolar diagnosis, but he agrees with the anxiety diagnosis. This struck me as funny since the last two doctors we had seen said that Xanthe was definitely, without a doubt, bipolar and now this doctor and the one at the hospital for the evaluation, think he might not be. While it was funny, it also scared me. If those two doctors could be so wrong, then what are the chances that these two are right. I long for the day that mental illness can be diagnosed with a blood test.

The psychologist is definitely going with severe separation anxiety disorder, but he also said that Xanthe's symptoms resemble post-traumatic stress disorder even though there is no evidence of an event that would have brought this on. He was honest enough to say that he is unsure right now and that Xanthe's case is a complicated one. There are too many differing symptoms and there does not seem to be a connection yet. We have severe anxiety, depression, irritability, racing thoughts, fear of leaving me, mild audio and sensory hallucinations and a lot of paranoia. He informed that he would need to consult with someone and read up on these behaviors before he could come to a conclusion and establish a treatment plan. Until then we are going to continue with the anti-anxiety therapy and try to teach him some self-relaxation techniques that he can use to calm himself down. The psychologist did warn me though, that until we could get his medications right the self-relaxation techniques probably wouldn't work on their own.

In order for the psychiatrist to change the medications further testing was needed. The wait for the psychologist that the psychiatrist suggested is over a month, but this new psychologist said that he could perform the tests next week and we could then forward the results to the psychiatrist. Great news! The testing is about 700 true or false questions that Xanthe will have to complete. It is three different tests in all. One of the tests will have to be interpreted by a different doctor. I do not know how long it takes to get the results, but I am happy to be moving in the right direction. I am sure that if we could just name this illness then we could get Xanthe the help he needs. Maybe things are turning around after all.

I also talked to the doctor about my feelings of co-dependency. During the conversation it came up that I used to travel for my job. Just as recently as last January I had gone to Canada for 5 days and right before that to Texas for 3. Before that I had been traveling for a little over a year. Each time Xanthe stayed happily with my mom, Chris, his dad or a combination of all three. And he did attend school willingly while I was gone. This information confused the doctor even more. What could have changed in March that would cause Xanthe to go from completely happy when I was out of town, to unable to function when I was in the other room? The puzzle just became more confusing as we dug for information.

As I hung up, I realized how much better this doctor was than any of the previous ones. Xanthe may still be sick, but at least we were learning things and this doctor had concrete advice that we could actually use outside of his office. I will never understand what made me keep the appointment, but I thank God that I did. I am just glad it is Friday. Maybe we can have a semi-calm weekend and things will look better on Monday.

Bedtime was better tonight. We all stayed up to watch a movie and Xanthe's Benadryl kicked in near the end. He was out when his head hit the pillow.

SATURDAY SEPTEMBER 7TH

~ Xanthe and Chris got up early this morning and went 4-wheeling at some sand dunes they had found. Tahni and I headed in to visit my mom and see if any of Tahni's friends could play. Nothing went right with our visit. My mom's cable was out and I spent all afternoon on the phone with the cable company trying to fix it. Tahni called all of her friends, but none of them were home. Finally, we headed home about 4pm. We were hoping to get home before the boys so that we could spend some time alone together.

Once home and thankfully alone, we made ourselves some dinner and sat down to play cards. We were too busy talking to really pay attention, so the game dragged on and ended up taking all of our time. Finally, Tahni won. Shortly after that, the boys arrived home. Xanthe was in a weird mood. He had had fun, but a couple times he had gotten really anxious while riding. This made him a little clingy for the rest of the evening.

Chris' parents had called while Tahni and I were playing and I invited them over for a late dinner and a board game. Both his parents and his two sisters came. We all had a great time. Playing the board game got us all laughing pretty hard. For whatever reason, Xanthe was in a great mood while they were here, so we were all more relaxed than usual. The only down side to the evening was that I had forgotten that Chris had told his family that I had quit my job, because the thought of me getting fired because of Xanthe's condition embarrassed him. But for me the thought of having them think I had quit was harder. We had just got this new house and a new truck so I felt that it would look awfully irresponsible of me to quit without finding another job first. I felt and still feel that it makes more since that I was fired. But I also respected Chris' view on things and understood why he had lied. I also knew that we would tell them the truth eventually, and that they would understand. Needless to say, the discussion about my new job was a little awkward.

Since it was so late when everyone left, we were all tired. Xanthe took his medication and then we cuddled on the sofa while Tahni and Chris headed to bed. About an hour later Xanthe was deep in sleep.

SUNDAY SEPTEMBER 8TH

~ I woke up first today and decided to surprise everyone with a good home-made breakfast. I had been slacking in the cooking department lately. I made pancakes, scrambled eggs with *cheese*, sausage and toast. Everyone loved the food and we had fun talking and joking with each other.

Chris and Xanthe decided to go riding again today. This time they went to a different spot and weren't gone as long. Tahni and I still had fun though just hanging out together. We even went out to eat hamburgers without the boys.

Xanthe was in a great mood all day. He didn't have any problems while riding. Once home, he and Tahni played air hockey and didn't argue once!

I was optimistic that his mood would last through bedtime, but as I headed in to the laundry room to put the clothes in the dryer Xanthe followed me. I could physically feel my body tense up as I asked him what was up. Immediately his face twisted up and the tears began to fall. I spent about twenty minutes trying to calm his fears. Tonight he was scared that he would never be able to go to school and that he would be a failure at everything he tried. I tried all my usual responses and encouragements and when that didn't work I gave him some Benadryl. Chris and Tahni again, headed to bed without us. I plopped down on the sofa with Xanthe and held him while he cried. Eventually he fell asleep. At first, I was too mentally drained to get up, but eventually I found the strength to move us off the sofa and into bed.

MONDAY SEPTEMBER 9TH

~ Today was bad again. Tahni went to school with no problem but Xanthe was upset from five o'clock in the morning on. I tried what the psychologist suggested and got in the car without him. Xanthe didn't even try to follow me. He just cried and said he was sorry.

After I dropped Tahni off at school I went to the middle school. I asked to talk to the counselor so that I could give her the information from the psychologist and explain why Xanthe wasn't coming in today. She was just as inconsiderate and rude as usual. The principal soon joined us and he was more understanding. I retold my story and he offered to come to the house and pick Xanthe up for school each day. I asked him what would happen if Xanthe crouched on the floor crying and throwing up. The principal explained that he would not legally be able to lift Xanthe up and force him into the car, but that he could try to talk him into going. I really didn't see how that would help since Xanthe becomes even more upset with strangers, but I was grateful that he was at least offering suggestions. The counselor had a few suggestions of her own. After I said I was at a loss as to what to do, she stated "Well, obviously you only have a few options. One, you can hospitalize him, two you can make him come to school or three you can home school him. But you need to decide soon, because if he continues not to show up for school then we are going to call social services and you could be charged with truancy."

Well, isn't she just the most helpful person in the world. First of all, I had told her numerous times that they do not just hospitalize your child because you ask them to and secondly, I would make him go to school if I could. Wasn't that why I was in here talking to them in the first place. The principal stepped in and offered a solution. He said that as long as Xanthe was on school grounds they wouldn't turn me in, yet. What this turned out to mean was that I was going to sit in the parking lot for seven hours with Xanthe tomorrow if I couldn't get him into the building. It seemed crazy that it would count toward attendance, but I was willing to try anything.

Before I left the principal walked outside with me to point out the three places where I could park my car. Two were in front of the building, one was in the back. The back was were the teachers parked, so I chose a spot out front. As I headed to my car, he waved and yelled out, "I will come check on you two in the morning."

I felt like an idiot as I waved back. He was being great about the entire ordeal, but I felt like a fool for having to have him come met me in the parking lot. Hopefully it wouldn't come to that!

On the way home the reality of tomorrow hit me and I started laughing out loud. Now, I was going to be the crazy mom sitting in the parking lot in ninety-degree weather with a kid that wouldn't go to school. If everyone thought that me sitting in room 103 was bad, wait until they saw this.

Xanthe was still upset when I got home. I almost cried when I saw his tear stained face watching me pull into the driveway. I was gone longer than he thought I would be. He had sat in the garage with the dogs while he waited for me to come home, hoping that they would protect him.

Once I got Xanthe inside, I explained to him what I had found out at the school. He started crying again. He was hysterical thinking that I would go to jail. He kept apologizing for making me go to jail. I tried to stress the parking lot idea, but he was stuck on jail. I dropped the subject for awhile and later when he was calmer we talked about sitting in the parking lot together. We decided that was to be the plan for tomorrow. It just gets weirder and weirder, doesn't it?

Bedtime was bad as expected. Xanthe had been upset all evening. Even the Benadryl didn't help. We spent another night on the sofa, this time discussing the drawbacks to sitting in the parking lot.

TUESDAY SEPTEMBER 10TH

~ Tahni got up and around with no problems. I think her session with the psychologist must have helped her deal with her feelings a little better because this was the third day that she went without a fuss.

Xanthe was a little slower to get around, but eventually we were all in the car and there were no tears in sight. I dropped Tahni off at school and smiled as I said, "If you need me today, tell the nurse I won't be home, but that she can find me in the middle school parking lot!" This made her laugh as she walked inside.

Sitting in the parking lot wasn't as bad as I thought it would be. I had brought a book to read, and I had made Xanthe bring his geography book. We sat and read for hours. The only hard part was enduring the stares we received from curious parents and knowing teachers. I tried to keep my head down most of the time.

After about three hours of sitting and thinking, I had had enough. Even if the school was ok with this idea, I was not. We should at least be doing some make-up work or something. What was he learning out here with me? I turned to Xanthe and explained that this was not going to work. We only had two choices now. Go to school or home school. He tried to answer right away, but I told him to think about it. I then pulled out of the parking lot and headed home. All day long I pointed out the pros and cons to each option.

By dinnertime, Xanthe claimed he had come to a decision. He was going to go to school tomorrow no matter what. A part of me wanted to believe him, but another part knew it was just wishful thinking. I supported him though, and never let on that I had any doubts. He made a big production of setting out his school clothes, organizing his back pack and finishing his make-up work. His busy hands gave away his fears as they shook through each task. I have to admit though, that he seemed very determined to follow his decision through.

Bedtime went fairly well, considering what was in store for tomorrow. Xanthe was upset about failing and still worried about jail so we talked about it for awhile and he eventually fell asleep.

WEDNESDAY SEPTEMBER 11ᵀᴴ

~ Today was my day to come to a decision. Xanthe was way out of control this morning. More fear and tears than ever before. He followed me around the house repeating his plea, "Please, just one more day. I know I can do it tomorrow. I just need one more day. Please!"

I decided right then and there that this decision was out of our control. Why was I trying so hard to make him do something he couldn't yet do? Knowing that eventually we would have a name for his illness and the right therapy and medications to go along with it,

I decided to pull Xanthe out of school. I thought this decision would make Xanthe feel better, but it caused him to cry harder. For the rest of the day, he switched between crying and anxious and crying and sad. He was upset that he had failed, that he wouldn't have the opportunity to make friends, that he wouldn't be like everyone else, that he had let everyone down.

I left Xanthe at home long enough to go to the school and inform them of my decision and then to stop at the library to get some books on home schooling. The school staff took my decision in stride. I didn't ask for the social worker or the principal I just spoke with the secretary. I got the feeling that she knew this was coming and that she was a little relieved. She told me to bring in all of his books tomorrow and that she would have a check waiting for me for the balance of his lunch account. That made me laugh. I had forgotten that I had put money in the account at the beginning of the year and that Xanthe hadn't eaten lunch at school even one time. The principal called me later to wish us luck. I got the feeling that he really did care how it all turned out.

All afternoon I dreaded informing Chris of my decision. Deep down I knew it was the only viable option we had left, but a part of me still felt like a failure. What if I had given up on Xanthe too soon?

I spent the evening glued to my new library books, writing down everything I thought might be important to my home schooling success. Chris was in a bad mood over the whole home schooling thing. He kept making comments about how easy the boy had it. I tried to tune him out because he was just voicing the same concerns I was trying to ignore.

Tahni was upset all evening about the decision too. Only, she was torn between wanting to go to school and wanting to stay home like Xanthe. A part of her wanted to go to school and make friends and have fun, but another part of her was a little jealous about the time Xanthe would get to spend with me and the fun things we might do while she was gone. I assured her that if I planned any fun "field trips," we would do them on Saturdays so that she could go along. This helped a little, but not much.

Xanthe had a rough time at bedtime. He was still very upset about the home schooling decision. Tahni and I stayed up with him half the night. I told Tahni that she should go to bed, but for whatever reason she needed to be close to me. I think we were all a little unnerved by the shift in our lives. We were about to start a whole new adventure and it made us all a little apprehension, all for our own reasons.

THURSDAY SEPTEMBER 12TH

~ Both Xanthe and Tahni had therapist appointments today. One at noon, the other at one. My original plan had been to take Tahni to school and then pull her out at eleven so we could make the appointment. We were both so tired from last night though, that we slept through the alarm and woke up at nine. Of course the minute that Tahni realized what had happened, she burst into tears. I just laughed a crazy little laugh while I thought about how out of hand this whole school-skipping thing was becoming.

The appointments went ok. I told the doctor about home schooling. He was not pleased. He said that we were allowing Xanthe to run away from his problems. I explained that I knew that, but I felt as though I had no choice. The last thing I wanted to add to my day was community service for truancy. He didn't laugh.

He did test Xanthe though, as planned. It wasn't as impressive as I thought it would be. The doctor handed Xanthe a lap top computer with the test opened on it and Xanthe answered true or false to about 170 questions. Some questions we had answered a hundred times before. *I have thought of killing myself. I get scared in certain situations. Being in large groups makes me anxious.* Other questions made Xanthe laugh. *I have flown across the Atlantic 30 or more times in the last month. I have not seen a car in the last ten years.* Xanthe answered false to both of these, but not before asking me what they meant. I just told him to answer the questions, I didn't want to sway his answers, but I found them odd myself.

After both sessions were over we made an appointment for next Thursday for Xanthe, but we didn't make one for Tahni. The psychologist felt that she was doing fine, but added that if she ever needed to talk to him again we could just make her another appointment. I asked him when he would have the results to the test and he assured me that we would know something by the end of next week.

We left and went across the street to eat Chinese food and make fun of the test. I wanted to eat out instead of heading straight home because I wanted to do something fun for a change. Sometimes we got so caught up in just trying to make it through the day that we forgot to stop and "smell the roses." After about twenty minutes of eating and laughing, we saw the doctor walk in. He came over to our table and we teased him about following us. He said that he had some preliminary results back about the test. It seemed that the findings pointed to a severe anxiety disorder. I nodded my head and thanked him. Privately, I wanted to scream. Did he really think he was telling me something new?

On the drive home, I kept thinking about the results of the test. I felt that we had just wasted an afternoon. I spent the rest of the day feeling defeated, let down and depressed. I had hoped the tests would come back with something concrete that we could use to make it all better. And if not better, than at least bearable. So much for hoping.

All night long the phone rang off the hook. Everyone had known that the testing was to happen today, so everyone was calling for the results. After about the tenth time of telling the story and it's depressing results, I got sick of the whole thing, turned off the phone and took a bath. The running water disguised my tears and I sobbed until my eyes were dry.

After my bath, I dosed Xanthe with Benadryl to ensure that he would sleep and waited for it to kick in. I just wanted to be alone with my thoughts and disappointments tonight. I did not have the energy to be strong for anyone else.

FRIDAY SEPTEMBER 13TH

~ Another crazy day. I am beginning to think that life can't get any worse. Tahni and I woke up at 7am and she got around for school. I left Xanthe sleeping in my room. The drive to school went well, but as we pulled up into the drop off line, she burst into tears. I pulled out of the line and into a parking space to find out what was wrong. She started begging me to home school her too. I grumbled in frustration and that caused her to cry harder. "Please don't be mad at me!" she begged.

I took a deep breath and went into reassuring mode. A mode I practically lived in. We talked in the parking lot for over an hour. She was very confused and frustrated. The whole mess was causing her to come unglued. I decided to drive home. I was too exhausted to force the issue in the parking lot and I couldn't really give her my full attention. My mind was obsessed with the thought that Xanthe might wake up and find out he was alone. The breakdown that would ensue as a result of that, was something I didn't even want to imagine, let alone live through!

Once at home, I made her sit down and write out a list of the pros and cons to home schooling. I informed her that whatever decision she made today, she would have to stick with. I did my parenting part by explaining that all decisions come with down sides, so she needed to keep that in mind when she reached her final decision. I also stressed to her that no matter what she decided, she would have days when she wished she had picked differently. It struck me as ironic, that now I was contemplating community service for the truancy of my daughter instead of my son. This was a first in our lives.

When she was done with her list, we went over it together. As I read it, parts of it made me laugh. Parts of the list were really grown-up and well thought out, other parts were typical of an eleven-year-old.

HOME SCHOOLING PROS-
I get to be with Mom all day
I get to sleep late
I get to go on fun field trips

HOME SCHOOLING CONS-
I have to be with Xanthe all day
I will not get to be with my friends
I will miss out on holiday parties
I will not get to go to after school clubs
No one will invite me to their birthday parties
I will be bored
My mom will have to work part of the time

SCHOOL PROS-
I get to hang out with my friends
No Xanthe
I get to go on cool trips and have fun parties
I get to join cooking club

SCHOOL CONS-
I will not be with my mom
I have to get up early
Sometimes I do not want to go

After we went over the list together, she wrote WINNER in big red letters by school. I asked her why she picked that one, and she stated that school had more pros and fewer cons. So very adult of her, I thought. After that was taken care of, she seemed better for the rest of the afternoon.

Xanthe and I did a little work on his math and then we all watched a show about tigers together. We had decided that tigers would be the first animal we would study for science, and that Xanthe would have to write a paper about what he learned. Tahni asked more questions during the show than Xanthe did, but I felt that we had all learned a lot by the time it was over. For the next few hours, I cleaned house and started dinner, Xanthe spent time on the Internet researching tigers and Tahni watched TV. It was a pretty cozy afternoon.

The psychologist called me today. I think that he must have sensed some of my disappointment yesterday. He had gone over the results again and wanted to share some more information with me. We spent about an hour on the phone while he explained Xanthe's anxiety, depression and mood swings. We discussed some triggers to these emotions, some techniques for avoiding them and some other techniques for getting through them when they did occur. I felt a hundred times better and more prepared when I hung up the phone. I was really beginning to like this doctor.

Tonight we had a break-through of sorts. Xanthe wasn't tired when the rest of us were ready for bed so he decided he was going to try to stay up for awhile by himself. Usually, I do not allow him to try this because he ends up hearing something and I have to stay up all night with him trying to calm his fears. But before I could say "no," I remembered what the doctor had said about Xanthe learning to deal with his anxieties. I needed to allow him to be in scary situations if he was ever going to learn to deal with them. Since he was no longer going to school, I needed to find other opportunities to do this. When I stated that he could stay up, everyone looked at me as if I was crazy. Once in bed, Chris informed that he thought I was nuts. "Don't you realize what is going to happen?" he asked. "Now, you will be up half the night with him."

We went to sleep sort of mad at each other. About an hour later Xanthe came into my room. He was scared. He swore he heard someone walking in the hallway. I reassured him that no one was there. I asked him if he wanted to go check and then come back and let me know. This was the psychologist's idea. Xanthe said no, so I asked him if he wanted me to lay down next to him. Of course, he said yes. I got us both settled in and closed my eyes thinking that this was going to be a long night. To my surprise I didn't wake up until eight o'clock the next morning. Xanthe had slept through the night!

SATURDAY SEPTEMBER 14ᵀᴴ

~ I went to the grocery store alone today. As I walked through the aisles, I felt strangely content. I chalked it up to one of two things. Either I had finally lost my mind, or our lives were getting a little better. As I slowly pulled things off the shelves, I realized that life had gotten a little better. Tahni was feeling better about going to school, I no longer had to fight with Xanthe and the school every day, I was studying to work at home and life seemed to have slowed down a little. I was even looking forward to tonight. Xanthe was going to his dad's so that they could fish, Tahni was having a friend spend the night and for awhile, I was going into town to spend time with my mom and sister. That last thought caused me to pick up two cards so that I could jot down a note of thanks to each of them for helping me through the hell of the last couple of months. I never understood how they found the time to live their lives and mine, but I was deeply grateful that they did it. They definitely deserved more than a card.

Once at home I unloaded the groceries and loaded in Xanthe's fishing gear. Both kids were ready to go. Chris had already left to go riding, so I locked the door and we headed into town.

I dropped Xanthe off at his dad's, picked up Tahni's friend and went to my mom's, where we spent a wonderful two hours. The girls played outside and I got to sit and talk about nonsense! It was a nice break from the usual harried routine.

I continued my lazy pace once we were home. Tahni and her friend went out to jump and swim, and I actually sat down to read a book. Not a book about home schooling or parenting techniques, but a regular book about someone else's life that I could lose myself in.

Once Chris came home, I made dinner, then we all watched a movie. The evening flew by without any incidents or tears. I even went to bed at the same time as Chris. I snuggled into his arms and went to sleep feeling safe and content.

SUNDAY SEPTEMBER 15TH

~ I woke up with the sun, feeling better than I had in a long time. I didn't even have to convince myself to get out of bed. I jumped up, showered and made breakfast, all before the girls woke up.

Since the girls were playing happily, I decided to hang out with Chris. He was in the garage working on his tractor. Our conversations were a little strained. We were both trying to avoid any discussions that would lead to arguments. Eventually, we settled into a nice groove and had a good time. I was in charge of retrieving the tools. More often than not, I brought him the wrong thing, but he stayed patient and I enjoyed the stress free chore.

Since Xanthe was staying at his dad's one more night, Chris, Tahni and I decided to do something other than just sit in front of the TV after her friend went home. About one o'clock, we all piled in the car and went for a drive. We spent hours just talking and laughing and discovering all the things we lived by. We found a small town when we ran out of gravel roads and ended up grabbing lunch (dinner?) out. It was a cool little "mom and pop place" complete with checkered tablecloths. We ordered huge sundaes to celebrate our yummy find. With full tummies, we headed home to watch another movie. It was fun and relaxing.

The whole day ended up solidifying my ideas of an improvement in our lives. It also helped that I had called Xanthe twice and he seemed to be doing great. I asked his dad how last night had gone and he said Xanthe had slept through the night. Before bed, while I brushed my teeth, I said a quick pray of thanks. I felt truly blessed.

MONDAY SEPTEMBER 16ᵀᴴ

~ Tahni went to school without a single problem today. I think she is pretty comfortable with her decision. She was all smiles and laughs as she exited the car and rushed to catch up with her friends. I felt tears spring to my eyes as I watched her. It felt great to see her happy.

I spent the first hour at home at a loss. With Xanthe at his dad's, I was all alone. It felt weird and I couldn't decide what to do. Finally, I decided to head outside. I sat out on our deck for hours just enjoying the sun and the quiet. I let my mind wonder over all the possibilities that these last few "good" days offered. *Could it be too much to hope that we had found something that worked?* A sliver of doubt tried to push its way into my mind, but I didn't allow it.

After I drove into town for Xanthe and then picked Tahni up from school we relaxed, made dinner and then played a game. The evening played out without a single hitch. Our lives felt almost normal.

As I enjoyed our quiet and calm evening, that same doubt from earlier resurfaced in my mind. This time I couldn't ignore it. Thanks to our new psychologist, I knew more about Xanthe's condition and I had a few techniques to use in a crisis, but I was still feeling very unprepared. Taking away school had taken away a big concern, but what happens when the next feared thing arises? Were we really making progress? Were we really working toward a solution or were we just practicing damage control?

TUESDAY SEPTEMBER 17TH

~ Tahni's morning was a repeat performance of yesterday. All smiles again as I dropped her off and waved good-bye.

Home schooling was a different story, entirely. It just might be a bit more than I had planned for. I had spent time on the Internet and at the library yesterday planning our lessons and printing out worksheets. Even with all the preparation, the whole thing was hard to get used too. The whole day was awkward as I went through each lesson. We had yet to find our groove. I was also a little discouraged at how far behind his grade level he was. All of the information I had printed out and prepared for a seventh grader was way over his head. He didn't even get one word correct on his spelling pre-test. I started adding in easier words as I saw what he was writing. Even those were too hard for him. He spelled family "famle" and about "abot". Finally, I gave up and called it a day. He went out to ride his four-wheeler for "gym" class and I went back online in search of fifth grade units and lessons. Hopefully, with the one-on-one attention I will be giving him all year, we will be able to work quickly and move up closer to a seventh or even eighth grade level. Or maybe I am just dreaming. I do that a lot!

On a brighter side, Xanthe seems to be doing better every day. I don't know if it is the medication change, the therapy or the fact that he stays home now, but whatever it is our lives are definitely getting

147

better.

Xanthe wasn't tired when we were tonight, but he wasn't brave enough to try staying up by himself again. Instead, he lay in bed next to me wiggling, tossing and turning trying to find a comfortable spot. Every five minutes he would whisper to me. Sometimes it was a question, sometimes it was just the ramblings of a bored child. Luckily, it was never any fears. After hours of this, he finally fell asleep.

WEDNESDAY SEPTEMBER 18TH

~ Tahni did great again this morning. This time she got around so quickly that she had extra time to work on her hair. After I oohed and aahed over numerous hairstyles, she finally decided on one to wear.

Xanthe was still asleep when I got back from taking Tahni to school and I let him sleep in. I selfishly wanted some time to myself. I took advantage of the quiet and sat in the living room looking out the huge picture window. The way the window is situated makes it appear as though we are the only house for miles. All you can see is beautiful green trees and rolling hills. It's so quiet, peaceful and planned. Through the window everything happens as it's supposed to. Crops grow, weather changes, leaves turn. It's all so predictable, so stable. I long for that kind of peace and routine in my life. The arrival of the mailman ruined the moment for me. He sped past my window in his old beat up black truck (no official mail jeeps way out here), spinning up dust and causing all the animals to bark and neigh. For a minute or two, real life had imposed on my daydream, but soon the dust settled and all was quiet again. I stole a few more moments before I went to wake Xanthe trying to recreate the peace I had felt, but the magic was gone.

Home schooling went better today. I am slowly beginning to feel better about this decision. Without the anxiety of going to school, Xanthe seems better able to concentrate and learn. And the fact that our mornings start out calmer, puts me in a better mood also. The switch to fifth grade material was a godsend. Xanthe did much better with his new set of spelling words and the math concepts were a lot easier for him to grasp. All in all, we accomplished a lot. He didn't even argue when I assigned him homework to do!

We had another therapy appointment today. We learned some more techniques for Xanthe to try when his anxiety ran high. I also learned a few new ways to deal with Xanthe and the different situations that life brings. I wish we had found this kind of therapy years ago, this behavioral therapy. I will no longer have to stand there feeling helpless when Xanthe loses control. I will no longer have to second-guess myself either. I will know that what I am doing is right, right for us anyway! I think that having that kind of confidence makes all the difference in these situations. The biggest thing we learned today is called "self-talk therapy." For this technique, Xanthe has to talk to himself with "good" phrases while the "bad" phrases run through his mind. The idea is that eventually the good phrases will push the bad ones out of his mind. It takes practice and will work better right now on small fears or if we catch the mood right away. When Xanthe is in a good mood, I am supposed to make him practice. We are to say things like... *I am lucky to have a lot of land, I am a great fisherman, My life is good,* and *I like myself,* together. I am hoping that if he says these things enough, we can train his brain to think positively. For now, though, it is just nice to have something to practice, something that feels like progress.

We had a chance to practice our new skills at bedtime. We had accidentally caught the tail end of the evening news and the story was about the murder of a child. Xanthe soon became convinced that he was next. I tried my usual technique of explaining why that wasn't possible, but as usual it didn't work. Next, we tried the deep breathing followed by the positive self-talk. It didn't work quickly, but it did eventually help. While repeating the phrases about the land and fishing, Xanthe latched onto an idea for a new fishing lure. We spent another hour discussing the logistics of production and a pricing plan. I was exhausted, but this train of thought was better than the alternative, so I played along. Thankfully, he talked himself out and finally fell asleep.

THURSDAY SEPTEMBER 19TH

~ Today went fairly well. We started our morning with a practice session of relaxation techniques then moved on to schooling. Xanthe, again, did better with the fifth grade materials and we spent a lot of time on science. We are studying fire and I had prepared an experiment. I figured that the hands on stuff would be right up his alley. He loved it so much we had to do it twice.

At 3pm, I left Xanthe at home while I went to pick up Tahni then go to the store. That was the plan anyway. I had no sooner pulled into the school parking lot, when my cell phone rang. It was Xanthe. He heard people in our garage. He told me that I had to come home right away. I explained that I couldn't, but that we could do his techniques over the phone. We tried them all, but nothing worked. Finally, after the longest 15 minutes known to man, Tahni came running out to the car. I raced home while still talking to Xanthe on the phone. Later, Tahni and I laughed about the ride home. High speed and gravel roads do not mix. Plus, I was driving with only one hand, the other one busy holding my lifeline to Xanthe. My driving was something akin to a race car driver on a very bad day. Maybe a race car driver who is blindfolded and has one arm tied behind his back on a very bad day. The car bumped and skidded on every turn. I am surprised we made it.

Once we arrived home, Xanthe was easy to calm down with the techniques we had learned. Maybe it was just too soon to expect him to do them while home alone. "Baby steps," I had to remind myself. In the end, we all ended up going to the store together. At least we had plenty of conversation for the way there. Tahni couldn't stop teasing me about my driving.

Xanthe was anxious for the few hours following his break down, but by the time Chris came home he was completely calm. I headed to the kitchen to make dinner and both kids offered to help. I was making stuffed pasta (stuffed with what? Duh, CHEESE!) so I gave the kids the fun jobs. While I boiled the noodles and stirred the sauce, they chopped the fresh herbs and diced the garlic. Dinner turned out great!

As bedtime drew closer, I could sense Xanthe's anxiety starting to rise. Before it had a chance to get out of control, I dragged him into the other room and we started in with the relaxation techniques. Once his breathing was controlled, we moved on to the self-talk. It did the trick and with the help of some Benadryl, Xanthe was out before I was.

FRIDAY SEPTEMBER 20TH

~ The days are going great now, as long as I do not leave Xanthe at home by himself. I can shower now without him standing outside the door. I can clean the house without him shadowing my every move. He can go outside to play without me having to go and watch him. Everyday things are a lot easier to accomplish. He still gets anxious and sad, but when these feelings start to come over him, he lets me know and we use his self-talk techniques until the mood passes. They seem to be working great! It seems that everyone on the message boards may have been right. I had read a million times that when you finally find a treatment (medication and therapy) that works the difference in your child is like night and day. I guess I was just never expecting it to really happen for us!

Home-schooling is right on track. The math is still tricky, but science and spelling are moving along just fine. We just finished reading a pretty good book and instead of writing a book report about it Xanthe wants to make a newspaper using the story line. I am excited to see how that turns out.

Tahni is still doing great with school. She even has a new best friend. The two of them spent the evening on the phone planning a sleep over and gossiping about their classmates. Watching Tahni's animated face made me smile.

We did have a rough start to bedtime. Xanthe was upset about his 4-wheeler track. He was bored with it and overly worried that he would never get a better one. And of course, if he never got a better one then he could never get better at riding. And if he never got any better, how was he supposed to race professionally? Before this train of thought could overcome him and turn into a night of gloom, I started one of his new relaxation techniques. This technique did not work the way it was supposed to, but it ended up helping just the same.

For this particular technique he was supposed to stand quietly and imagine his body relaxing. I was supposed to lead him through this process. The first step was to take a deep breath. The instructions read: Breath through the soles of your feet. As soon as I said it we both erupted into laughter. We then spent the next 30 minutes trying to breathe through our feet. Xanthe sat down, held his feet up in the air and yelled, "Help, I am suffocating, when I stand up, my feet can't breath."

We never really did relax, but the laughter did drive away the gloom. After that he was easy to settle down and we all went to sleep with ease.

SATURDAY SEPTEMBER 21ST

~ Today was a great day. We did not have any major blow ups and the day sped by. I did burn our breakfast, but that was becoming routine to my family, so we just laughed it off and ate cereal. Xanthe made a comment about cereal not containing any cheese. I threatened to slice some up for him, but he pulled his bowl away!

The kids spent the afternoon swimming and jumping with the neighbor's kids. Chris kept busy in the garage and I was supposed to be doing housework. I cheated though. With all of them busy, I sneaked into the living room and watched two hours of cooking shows. It was awesome. Eventually, I pulled myself away from the TV and did the dishes. I wanted it to look like I had accomplished something with my time!

Later we went to dinner at Chris' parent's house. We spent six hours eating, talking and playing board games. It was just like last time, only better. Xanthe and I were even more relaxed this time. Not once did he become anxious or obnoxious. I got to play the game instead of playing referee.

Bedtime was kind of tricky. Maybe it was because we were out so late and Xanthe was overly tired. Xanthe was convinced that a burglar was waiting in the basement. He had an entire story prepared for how the guy had gotten in and what he was planning to do when we fell asleep. The relaxation techniques and self-talk didn't work, so finally I just had him lay down and I drew on his back while I told him fishing stories. This was a trick I had used numerous times over the years and I still resorted to it now and again. As I began the story, I would draw the scene I was describing. I always made him the main character and I drew every detail. I would draw the lake, the sky, the boat, him, his pole and tackle box. Then using my fingers I would act out the actions of the scene I was describing. I made the fish swim, the boat rock and the line spin in. When I felt his breathing even out, I lead him to bed.

SUNDAY SEPTEMBER 22ND

~ Today was another great day. I made my famous homemade waffles. Everyone ate until they were sick. It was fun hanging out in the kitchen with Tahni and making breakfast while we listened to the boys talk about cars. As I was beating the egg whites, I stared at my family and tried to commit the scene to memory. We were a picture of normalcy. I wanted to remember this moment forever.

After breakfast, we all headed outside to play. First, we played horseshoes. I was on Xanthe's team and we lost to Chris and Tahni. After one game the kids were bored, so Chris and Xanthe decided to ride the track and Tahni and I went swimming. It was pretty warm out and soon the boys had parked the bikes and Xanthe joined us for a swim. We raced, splashed and dove for sticks before I threw in the towel.

I left them swimming and headed in to make dinner. It was still nice out, so we decided to barbecue. Xanthe hopped out long enough to light the grill. I watched them swim and do tricks as I grilled the burgers and hot dogs. We ate out on the deck and finished up just in time to watch the sun set. It was a beautiful day.

Bedtime was the same tonight, only different. Xanthe was anxious again. Something about serial killers. This time though he tried using the relaxation techniques by himself. I kept glancing over at him while I pretended to read my book. I could see that he was struggling to relax, but the look of determination on his face convinced me that he would succeed. Once he was calmer, we discussed topics he could think about in bed. I tried to steer the choices away from anything that could turn out scary. He finally settled on creating names for his band. I lay in bed for about an hour pretending to be asleep, listening for him and staying ready incase he needed me. He didn't. He slept the entire night through.

MONDAY SEPTEMBER 23RD

~ This morning was good again. I let Xanthe sleep in as Tahni got around for school. I didn't feel as anxious about leaving him as I usually did. Tahni was extra excited about school today. She was going to play her saxophone in front of the class.

Once home, I woke Xanthe. We did our self-talk and relaxation practice and then moved on to school. We got hung up on some new math techniques and ended up spending hours on that one subject. For homework, I assigned him new spelling words and he sat at the computer for awhile typing them out three times each.

Since I seemed to have more time on my hands lately, I decided to make a real dinner, not one that comes out of a box or contains cheese. All afternoon I worked in the kitchen. I marinated Bratz, I boiled potatoes and I made a cake from scratch. I sang while I cooked because I was so impressed with my rusty skills. I was celebrating way too early. By the time I set dinner on the table, it had all gone wrong. I had burnt the sausages so badly that they resembled charcoal briquettes more than food. I had not cooked the potatoes long enough so they were hard and inedible. The cake turned out great though, so we had an entire dinner based on cake and ice cream.

I am sure that if I tried hard enough, I could come up with some way to tie our dinner to all four-food groups. Milk is a protein, right? And I did use eggs in the batter!

Bedtime went well. With his new techniques, he was able to stay calm and get ready for bed without any fear or anxiety. I am afraid to get used to this. I couldn't sleep because I was waiting for things to go wrong. It had been too many nights that Xanthe had slept all night. I ended up getting up and reading in the living room until two o'clock. I haven't slept repeatedly all night in twelve years, so even if Xanthe sleeps all night I find that I can't. It is a habit for me now.

TUESDAY SEPTEMBER 24TH

~ Today Xanthe woke up grumpy. No matter what I said or did, he stayed mad about everything. We didn't have a thing to eat, we didn't have the pop he liked, it was too hot to ride, to sunny to fish, to everything to do anything! I finally gave up and headed to the computer to work.

After an hour or so I tried again. I reminded Xanthe of the steps he was supposed to take to talk himself out of a bad mood. We tried positive self-talk, we tried coming up with solutions to the things he deemed wrong, and we even tried some classical music. Who knew that one classical song could last 25 minutes? I am not sure which one did the trick, but his mood was lifted enough for us to get some schoolwork done. Later he rode his 4-wheeler and played with his friends.

In the shower later, I reflected back on the day. I liked our new ways of dealing with things. I still had to wonder though, if any of this would have been possible if he was still trying to go to school? *Could that be part of the key that brought this all together? And if so, did it mean that Xanthe wouldn't ever be able to go to school? Was I jumping ahead of myself?*

I think my anxiety from earlier might have carried over to Xanthe because he was a mess at bedtime. Grumpy and depressed again. I tried to get him to go through his techniques with me, but he didn't give them much effort. He was convinced that they wouldn't work. All of his thoughts were negative. He hated life. He didn't go to school, he didn't have any friends his own age, he was a terrible drummer and so on. Every topic I brought up led him to new gloom. I finally gave up and turned on the TV. I found some infomercials, dragged Xanthe to the sofa and listened to him predict dire outcomes while I waited for his mood to pass. Eventually, a commercial for a new trash can caught his attention and his thoughts turned down a new avenue. For the next half hour we debated the pros and cons of this inexpensive purchase. Soon his eyelids grew heavy and his speech slowed down. Fifteen minutes later I was able to lead him to bed.

WEDNESDAY SEPTEMBER 25TH

~ The doctor called me today. He had found a book he thought Xanthe and I should read. It was all about changing the habit of being afraid. I went to the library and checked it out. It's a great book written for people who suffer from extreme anxiety. The point of the book is to slowly replace feelings of fear in a situation with other, stronger feelings. The author insists that fears are partly a learned behavior that start small and then cumulate by habit into something uncontrollable. That really makes a lot of sense.

We tried a few of the techniques today and we were impressed. I had Xanthe lay still with his eyes closed and relax. Once he was relaxed, I started to describe in great detail his returning to school. I described our drive to the school, where we parked, our walk through the double glass doors. I kept on with this imagery until he was standing with his teacher and I was heading for the door. That is when his finger came up. The book had suggested that as the signal to use when you were becoming anxious. At that point, I reminded Xanthe that he was still in the school with the teacher, but that he could feel safe. I instructed him to relax his muscles. I rubbed his shoulders for effect. I reminded him to breathe deeply. In between calming instructions, I would remind him that he was still at school, but not as afraid. Eventually, I got him to a point where he could imagine being in the school and still be calm. At that point, I described leaving with me for the day. We had to stop and start this technique quite a few times until we finally got to the point of no fear, but it was well worth the effort.

Now according to the book, I am supposed to keep adding steps to this until he can imagine staying relaxed in the classroom for a full day. With enough practice, this will enable him to transfer these feeling of calm to the actual event by habit when he comes in contact with it. I plan on informing the therapist about our progress and seeing if he wants to continue this same treatment at our sessions. I think we might be onto something here.

Bedtime was great. Xanthe was in a hyper mood for most of the evening, but around ten he crashed. He sat down to watch TV and fell asleep in his chair. All I had to do was lead him to bed.

THURSDAY SEPTEMBER 26ᵀᴴ

~ Another great day! Tahni had a wonderful time at school. Xanthe and I started studying the civil war. (Don't tell anyone, but I think he already knows more than I do. It has been way too long since I studied this stuff!) Chris had a great day at work and I just smiled all day because everyone seemed so happy. It had been days since Xanthe's last severe anxiety attack. He had slept all night again last night, so that made 5 nights in a row. That hadn't happened since the beginning of sixth grade! I also took a real bath before bed. Not a quick bath while Xanthe was crying at the door, not an escape bath were I cried the entire time, but a real bath, meant only for cleansing and relaxation.

I made a big production of the entire thing. I lit candles and I brought a glass of pop in to enjoy while bathing. (I know most people would have brought wine, but keep in mind my pop addiction!) I stood in front of the mirror for a second while my water ran and thought about all the blessings in my life. I saw a smile spread across my face. The smile looked good there. So good that I had to stare.

Eventually, I pulled myself away from my reflection, turned out the lights and soaked in the tub until the water turned cool. I did almost cry at one point, but not because I was sad. I almost cried with the joy I was feeling about our lives right now. Life actually seemed to be coming together for us. I sat in the warm water and let my mind run wild. *Could we have found what works for us? Is this the beginning of a real life for all of us? Can this be the magic combination of medication, therapy and family effort that works to keep Xanthe even and happy?* For the first time in what seemed like forever, I was not afraid of what tomorrow might bring. If anything I was looking forward to it! I leaned back into the water and relaxed. Truly relaxed.

FRIDAY SEPTEMBER 27ᵀᴴ

~ I woke up this morning with a feeling of unease. It took me a moment to place it. It suddenly dawned on me that I didn't know what to do now. For twelve straight years my mind has constantly been thinking ahead to the next crisis, the next breakdown, the next fight. I did not know what to think about now. It's very hard to explain. I can only compare it to what it must feel like a few weeks into retirement. When you finally come to the realization that this is not just a vacation, this is the rest of your life. For years you have based your life around a certain routine and now that routine is gone. In a way, you have to reinvent your life. That is how I felt when I woke up and the thought scared me, yet excited me. I was scared of the uncertainty of it all, but excited about the possibilities it held. I bounded out of bed, ready to take on this new adventure called life.

My mood changed when later, I was sitting on the deck watching the sun set and I realized that we still had a lot to overcome. We still had yet to finish Xanthe's testing and hopefully get a name for his symptoms. His dad and I had decided to go ahead with the extensive testing at the "not-covered by insurance" hospital since the last testing was a dud. I still had yet to teach a seventh grader everything he should have learned in the fifth and sixth grades. Chris and I still had yet to survive the trip through puberty with two kids. We had a lot to do. Yet none of this scared me anymore. For the first time in twelve years, I felt somewhat prepared to take it all on. Would it be easy? No. But now I had some of the tools necessary to see it through. I may not always get it right, but at least I was headed in the right direction. With the deep breath of a confident mom, I stood up and headed inside. I was actually looking forward to spending the evening with my family!

Just as I expected, the evening went well. We ordered pizza, played cards and laughed until our stomachs hurt. Around nine, Chris, Tahni and I settled down to watch TV and Xanthe went to his room to practice his techniques. By ten, everyone was relaxed and ready for bed. I tucked Xanthe and Tahni in and then crawled in next to Chris. Bedtime was so easy now. I was still dreading the day that we bought a new bed and I had to move the kids out of our room, but for now I was enjoying the peace that this situation offered.

SATURDAY SEPTEMBER 28TH

~ Life is moving along quite smoothly. Tahni is happy at school. Xanthe is happy at home. Chris is happy with our progress. I am happy to be happy. I do have one reservation, though. I am beginning to wander if things are running smoothly because we never go out anymore. Since I home school Xanthe, he never has to leave me or the house. I am afraid I might be falling into yet another pattern. The first one was submission. Is this one avoidance? And if so, is it an actual choice on my part or is it an effect of circumstances? I think I need to sign Xanthe up for something that he needs to leave home for or schedule another family gathering. Anything to shake things up a bit. If we don't try, how will we ever know if we are truly making progress?

Other than my new found worry, today went great. The kids got along well and Chris and I spent sometime reconnecting on the deck. As the evening wore on, our stomachs began to grumble. I was feeling too lazy to make dinner, so we piled in the car and went out to eat. We tried a new place in the next town over and it turned out to be great. On the way home we rented a movie.

Bedtime was easy again. Xanthe and I sat down to run through the relaxation techniques. This time Tahni decided to join us. Xanthe took great pride in explaining the process to her and leading her through the steps. This new twist gave him something different to concentrate on. He was so busy directing Tahni that he forgot to be scared. When we finished we headed to bed without a single problem.

SUNDAY SEPTEMBER 29ᵀᴴ

~ Today was another good day. Chris and Xanthe spent the day in the garage bringing an old tractor back to life. I went out a few times pretending to look for something just to sneak a peak at how well they were getting along. Ever since things have improved with Xanthe, he and Chris have been getting along great. I can almost see the layers of resentment peeling away. Chris is having fun teaching Xanthe the mechanical basics and Xanthe is having a great time learning. Chris even compliments him on a job well done and thanks him for his help at the end of the day. This all leaves Xanthe beaming with pride. I am happy for both of them.

Since the boys were busy in the garage, Tahni and I decided to unpack some more of the house. We did our job slowly, lazily. It was nice to hang out without Xanthe shadowing our every move. One box we found left us side-tracked for over an hour. It was filled with old pictures. We moved closer together and looked at them all. We lost track of the present as I told her the stories of our past that were captured in the photographs. As I talked, I would sneak glances at her out of the corner of my eye. She was growing up. It was hard to find my baby in the layers of golden hair and the newly formed mature features of her face. I was suddenly overcome with a need to hold her, to keep her in this moment. She interrupted my thoughts with a question. "What is this?" she whispered.

She had found a card I had bought for myself years ago. At first the card was for inspiration, but reading it now brought out feelings of life's truths. On the front of the card there is a picture of a little girl with her suitcase walking down the left side of a fork in the road. Behind her, in the center of the fork, is a pole with two street signs attached to it. The sign pointing in the direction she has decided to travel states *YOUR LIFE*. The sign pointing in the opposite direction states *NO LONGER AN OPTION*. Reading it gave me goose bumps. It seemed the perfect mantra for our lives. Tahni and I found an old frame, cut the card to fit and hung it in the living room for all to see.

Even with the day's earlier happy events, Xanthe was depressed by bedtime. All that time working on the tractor had made him want one for himself. Of course, he didn't have the money to buy one and neither did we. This led him to the conclusion that we were poor because I had lost my job because of him. This realization led to an even bigger sense of failure and his mood spiraled farther down. Tahni and I sat with him and started in with the positive self-talk. To my complete surprise, it actually worked. Within an hour, our repetition of positive sayings had led Xanthe to a discussion of finding a job on a neighboring farm. This led to him making plans for all the money he was going to make. In the time span of one hour, we went from total losers to budding entrepreneurs. It made my head spin.

TUESDAY OCTOBER 1ST

~ Sometimes things just fall into your lap. Xanthe's dad called today. He wants to take Xanthe to the speedway this weekend. He somehow managed to score tickets for qualifying on Friday and for races on both Saturday and Sunday. This means Xanthe will be gone from Friday afternoon to Monday morning. It is just the opportunity I was looking for. Xanthe will be away from me and the house, plus he will be hanging out with a group of friends and family. I said yes before we even discussed the details. I know that Xanthe will be thrilled with the idea, and I am anxious to take this step to see if he can make it.

Home schooling was crazy today. It wasn't the lessons or even teaching them that threw me off. It was more the entire concept. Science went fine. We studied sand dunes and their formation. We even made one with a hair dryer and some sand box sand. For social studies, we studied the people of the rain forest. We tied that in with their land for a unit in geography. Art and music were a snap. Math is what got me thinking. We had moved on to some sixth grade concepts and hit a wall. When I introduced equations involving fractions, he was lost. We ended up spending two hours on this. By the time I assigned his homework, I was feeling pretty good about his understanding. I was wrong. He struggled through each problem. So tomorrow I am going to re-teach the unit. In a nutshell, that is what scared me. *What if I can't teach this? Where do I turn from here?* It's not like I have other teachers to consult or even a learning center teacher to hand him over to. Teaching a "normal" child is one thing, but teaching a child with learning disabilities is quite another. People who do that have four years of training under their belts. I hope I haven't taken on more than I can handle. Once again, I have to wonder if my decision was fair to Xanthe. I just might lack the know how to pull this off. Back to the library I guess!

I lost my cool at bedtime tonight. Right after I announced bedtime, Xanthe stated that he was scared. I asked all of my usual questions. What are you afraid of? What are you thinking about? Did you see something scary today? Each question was met with, " I don't know." He was uneasy and he didn't know why. That frustrated me. *How I was supposed to calm him down if I didn't know what I was talking about? How could he have no idea what was bothering him?* After about an hour of 20 questions, three failed techniques and one frustrated blow up (mine), I finally gave up and reverted to my old ways. I dosed him with Benadryl, led him to bed and held him tightly until he fell asleep. Not very conducive to therapy, but I was too tired to care!

WEDNESDAY OCTOBER 2ND

~ Our math session went better today. After consulting with

Chris, I decided to break the lesson down a little more. This seemed to help and Xanthe managed to do most of the assigned problems by himself. I think I was just moving to fast.

We had another therapy appointment today. This one didn't go so well. They started out talking about fishing and somehow ended up talking about the government watching us all with little cameras. Xanthe was insisting that there were 30,000 cameras in our neighborhood alone. Then he tried to convince the doctor that some of these cameras were hidden in the quarters that he had in his pocket. Of course, the doctor was disagreeing with him. That made Xanthe angry. The more the doctor didn't believe, the angrier Xanthe became. The whole thing was very scary to watch. I had never realized how obsessed Xanthe could become. At home when he told his wild stories, we just assumed it was his great imagination at work and we went along with whatever he said so that we wouldn't crush his creativity. I never realized he could be so paranoid. When I didn't think I could take watching a second longer, the clock signaled that our time was finally up. I rushed Xanthe out of there before it could get any worse.

On the way home, Xanthe seemed shaken by the session, but didn't want to discuss it. He made nervous, awkward chatter for the entire drive, forcing away the silences. I let him. I didn't want to discuss what had happened yet either. I needed time to process it all.

Xanthe was quiet for the rest of the day and so was I. Chris and Tahni could sense that something was up, but they didn't ask and I didn't volunteer the information. We finished out the day with each of us just going through the motions, each caught up in our own thoughts and concerns.

Bedtime was horrible, but then I knew it would be. I figured that the anxiety from earlier would have to come out somewhere. This time though when I asked him which technique he wanted to try, he refused to do anything the doctor had taught us. He claimed that they were really brainwashing techniques. I knew Xanthe still trusted me, so I mentioned a game we used to play when he was little. We call it the "drawing on the back game." The minute Tahni heard me mention it, she wanted to play too. The game is very simple. You just have one person lie down on their stomach and the other players have to draw an object on their back for them to guess. Before each drawing though you have to give a clue. The clues can be anything from the object's color or size, to ways to use it. Of course, Xanthe wanted to guess first. Tahni and I took turns drawing a picture of a race car on his back and giving him clues. He whined that his turn had been too easy. We played for over an hour and the objects kept getting crazier and crazier. At one point I was the guesser, and for the drawing the kids just used the tip of their finger to draw a small dot on my back. My clues were…*it is gray, it is small, it likes TVs.* I had no idea ,so I had to give up. Amid giggles, I learned that the object was a piece of dust! I accused them of cheating, but that just made them laugh harder. The game was fun and it worked. Xanthe was calmer and he went to sleep easily. Sometimes you just have to be creative.

THURSDAY OCTOBER 3ʳᴰ

~ The first thing I did today was call the doctor. I wanted to see what he though about yesterday's appointment. He was more unnerved than I was. This was a side of Xanthe he had never seen before. I explained that we had seen the wild story side of Xanthe before, but since we never called him on it we never saw the upset, obsessed side. The doctor felt that this was a side to Xanthe that we needed to explore and work on. I, of course, agreed. If nothing else, the session answered two questions for me. Yes, Xanthe's home schooling was very much a part of why things were better and yes, we had a lot more work to do. We ended the call with the doctor agreeing to look into different treatments and with me being glad I had kept that other testing appointment. Obviously there was more to learn here.

Xanthe was in a better mood today. He seemed to be over the anxiety that yesterday had caused. His new mood was excitement. He talked non-stop about the upcoming races. Home schooling was hard because he was having trouble focusing. He kept wiggling in his chair, blurting out statements about race day, and doodling on his papers. Somehow we managed to get it all done. The minute I said we were finished, Xanthe flew from his chair announcing his intention to start packing.

Xanthe had trouble getting to sleep tonight. I think it was a combination of excitement and anxiety. He is really looking forward to the weekend, but he is very nervous about "freaking out" in front of everyone. I tried my best to console him, but soon I realized that this was one of those moments that a parent just has to let go and let their child face uncertainty alone. By facing his fears this weekend and overcoming them, hopefully he will feel better and more confident the next time something scary comes along. That said, I still wish I could help him every step of the way and I am afraid of how this weekend could turn out, but I am going to try to stay strong for his sake. If you are listening,God, we could use some help down here!

FRIDAY OCTOBER 4TH

~ Today is the day. Xanthe is running around like crazy. He keeps jumping from packing for the weekend to sitting by me for comfort. I can almost see the war of emotions going on behind his eyes.

Right after breakfast this morning we had another habit changing session. This time I used the races as his imagery. I was hoping that it would help later, if something came up. I wanted him to feel armed with the right tools to handle his anxiety this weekend. He did a lot better with this imagery than with the school scene. I think the anxiety that he feels about this weekend is lower than that of going to school. I am beginning to rate his fears by anxiety level so that I know which ones to work on first. The book says to start with the lowest and work your way up. We have a lot to work on.

We tried to work on school today, but Xanthe was so wound up that he wasn't learning anything. I would finish explaining a concept, question him on his understanding of it and find that he hadn't retained a word of it. After about an hour of this, I gave up and called it a day. I was tired of wasting our time.

We drove straight to town from Tahni's school. Xanthe was hyper for the entire drive. I didn't try to stifle his excitement, I was hoping that it would help him through the weekend. Tahni was excited also, but every time she tried to talk about it, Xanthe interrupted. Once at their dad's, I tried to cut our parting short. I didn't want to linger long enough for my uneasiness to rub off on Xanthe.

Once we were back in the car and headed home, "Tahni-fest" began. Another weekend where Tahni would be the star of the show. We laughed, played road games and listened to her favorite radio station.

After a dinner of beef stroganoff (Tahni's favorite), we all played Monopoly. Thankfully, Tahni won! By ten, everyone was worn out and ready for bed. I was tired too, but I didn't want to give in just yet. I was secretly waiting for the phone to ring. When it hadn't rung by eleven, I gave in and went to bed. Just to be safe though, I brought the phone in with me.

SATURDAY OCTOBER 5TH

~ Today was fun. Tahni and I spent most of the day planning her upcoming birthday party. We made out the invitation list, planned the games and chose a decoration theme. Then we headed to the store to buy a few things. After searching three party shops, Tahni couldn't find any invitations she liked. We finally decided that we would make them ourselves. We bought the supplies and headed home, but not before stopping off to have lunch, just the two of us.

With full bellies and all the time in the world, we settled in at the dining room table to create the invitations. We were having a blast stamping, coloring, cutting and gluing and time flew by. Before we knew it, it was time to clean up and start dinner. After another meal of Tahni's choosing, we relaxed on the sofa and watched a movie. When it was over we headed to bed.

I tucked Tahni in at 11pm, plopped down between her and Chris and let out a sigh of relief. Two days down and one more to go. Xanthe has been doing great. Of course, I have called a hundred times to check on him. A couple times he kept me on the phone for awhile. I could hear the fear in his voice, although he never admitted to it. The rest of the time though he was too busy to talk to me and I had to get my information from his dad. Bedtime had been rough both nights. His dad has had to sleep next to him and he hasn't fallen asleep before midnight either time. Days have been great though. He has stuck close to his dad at all times, but he seems to be having fun. They did have a rough patch earlier today. Xanthe started "freaking out" and was about ready to cry. His dad took a walk with him to get him away from the noise and the crowds and they spent some quiet time together just talking about the races. After about an hour, Xanthe seemed to have pulled it all together again so they headed back to join their friends. After that, Xanthe has been great. I guess he just needed a moment to calm down and regroup. *I have to wonder what calmed him down? Did he use the techniques he is learning or was it something else?* I need to remind myself to ask him because I want to keep track of everything that turns his moods around. I never know when I will need a fresh idea!

SUNDAY OCTOBER 6TH

~ I couldn't sleep at all last night. I kept worrying about Xanthe. When I did drift off to sleep for a few minutes, I would wake suddenly thinking I had heard the phone ring. It never did. I was also wound up about the testing scheduled for Monday. I was afraid of what we would learn. No, I take that back, I was afraid of what we wouldn't learn. I was afraid to be let down, afraid that Xanthe would be let down. Afraid that no one could help us. Even though life was going so much better now, I knew that we were still far from "normal." Other 12-year-olds do not sleep with their parents every night. Other 12-year-olds go to school. Other 12-year-olds have fun without the worry of death. While I was glad for the improvements, I truly wanted Xanthe to have a normal life. In bed at night when it is dark and quiet, I cry for all the things he is missing out on, I cry for the childhood he has lost and I cry for the future he may never have. You would think that after twelve years I would be out of tears, but each day brings a fresh set and a new reason to shed them.

After a yummy breakfast of pancakes and sausage, Tahni went out to play with our next door neighbor's daughter. I used the time to clean the house. As I was doing dishes, I realized something important. I am always sad and depressed when the kids are gone and I think I now know why. It is quiet without them and I have too much time to think. Too much time to reflect back on everything and dissect what I have done wrong. When the kids are home, my mind is in war mode and I am always busy trying to keep the upper hand. I need a hobby. Maybe that will keep me from my self-pity. All in all, life is good and I need to find a way to keep myself from obsessing about past events and future what ifs? I need to learn to live.

Our evening went well. I only heard from Xanthe once and he seemed to be holding it together. Tahni and I spent some more time together playing and cuddling. Chris and I even found a few minutes to talk and be alone. By bedtime, I was sleepy, but slightly anxious about tomorrow morning.

MONDAY OCTOBER 7TH

~ TESTING DAY!!! We arrived at the hospital at 8am in good spirits. The doctor came in, introduced herself and then asked Xanthe to join her down the hall for testing. I asked how long they would be. She thought it would take about 4 hours. I mentioned something about going to the cafeteria for some breakfast. Big mistake. That is when Xanthe lost it. I think I screwed up when I hinted to the fact that we might not be staying in the waiting room the entire time. He started crying and refused to go off alone. After some failed convincing on my part and the doctor's, she agreed to let me come with them. I wish I had kept my mouth shut about the cafeteria, but there was no taking it back now.

The testing went well, I think. It was very intense and in-depth. I sat in a chair pretending to read a magazine, but I was silently answering the questions along with Xanthe. I was surprised at how many we answered the same. I would say we agreed ninety percent of the time. He did shock me with a few of his answers. He stated that once he fell asleep, his rest was calm and uneventful. *Yeah right!* He also stated that he was never sad and always confident about his future. *What? Where had I been on these nights? Obviously with someone else's sad kid!*

His personality definitely came out during the testing. One part required him to look at black and white pictures and describe the scene he saw. His answers were very descriptive and animated. One description struck me as odd, though. The picture was of three people. A man, a woman (in what appeared to be a doctor's coat), and a little boy. The man and the woman were whispering to each other. Xanthe stated that the woman was a doctor and she was telling the dad that the little boy would need *death*-threatening surgery. Not life-threatening, but death-threatening. Odd choice of words, I think. The therapist then asked him to describe what everyone was feeling. The doctor was sorry, the dad was sad and the boy was happy because he did not know what was being said. He was daydreaming about fishing while they talked. I do not know what to think of that story, but I hope it gives them some insight!

After about an hour, I could tell that Xanthe had relaxed somewhat so I claimed I had to use the restroom. Really, I went down the hall to hang out with Tahni and her dad. I wanted to let them know what was going on and also give Xanthe and the doctor some privacy.

When I returned to the room, a different doctor was waiting to speak to me. I learned that she was the doctor that would be interpreting the tests and she needed some background information on Xanthe. She led me to a separate room so that we could talk privately. Again, most of her questions were routine, but she did ask me a few I had never heard before. *Did he stare at fans or light bulbs? Did he walk on his tip toes? Did he shake or wring his hands a lot?* No, to all of the above. When we started to discuss his present symptoms, I lost control. For some reason, I started to cry. I HATE when that happens. She asked me if I was tired. All I could do was nod my head. I felt like an idiot, especially since things had been going so well. *Where did these feeling come from?* She asked me a few more questions, more to let me save face then to get information, then headed out to talk to Xanthe's dad. I sat in the room for awhile trying to get my head together. I did not want to walk back in to Xanthe and have him see me upset.

All in all, today went well. We will not get the results back for weeks and then we will still have to make an appointment to see the psychiatrist to discuss them. I can wait though. I am just glad it is over. No matter what the verdict is, we are making progress and that is what really counts.

TUESDAY OCTOBER 8ᵀᴴ

~ We had a break through of sorts today. I was reading to Xanthe out of one of the therapy books and I came to a great example of how anxiety feeds on itself and how it can be stopped. This example used the idea of an electrified chair. The point of the story was that if you sat in a chair once and it shocked you, then every time after that when you came to that chair you would be nervous about getting shocked. If you were shocked ten times in a row, you would then avoid the chair. And if later, you were shown that the chair was unplugged and now safe, you would still be afraid to sit in that chair. Your thoughts of being shocked would be too strong to overcome the knowledge that the chair was unplugged. To beat this, you would have to slowly reintroduce yourself to the chair, until eventually you could sit in it with out even a fleeting thought of being shocked. As soon as I finished the last sentence, I could literally see a light come on behind Xanthe's eyes. It was as if for the first time he was understanding where his anxiety was coming from and the work involved to overcome it. The whole thing excited him and he began to ask me tons of questions about getting started. I think I might have just reestablished his belief in therapy. I called the therapist with the news. For the first time in twelve years Xanthe truly understood that a cure could come from inside him. I am not sure who was happier, me or the therapist!

Xanthe's new found confidence carried over to his school work. He seemed more motivated and interested today. We flew through each subject with minimal interruptions or arguments.

After we picked Tahni up from school , Xanthe was excited to share his new found insight about therapy with her. He explained the entire concept to her in accurate detail. It was heart-warming to watch. After the explanation, he *begged* to practice his techniques again. I almost fell over myself in my rush to get the books. We then spent an hour practicing all we knew. I was touched by the effort Tahni put into the whole thing, knowing that such effort had to be born of deep love and pure empathy. She is an amazing little girl.

Bedtime brought a request to practice once again. I am not sure if this was just an extension of the earlier excitement or if Xanthe was feeling anxious once again, but I readily agreed without pressing for an explanation. Tahni chose to join us and her involvement brought an added calm to our session. Once finished, it was a piece of cake to lead Xanthe to bed.

WEDNESDAY OCTOBER 9TH

~ With Xanthe's new found understanding of his illness, therapy went even better today. It was as if each exercise had new meaning and greater effect. I am glad it has finally clicked for him. His favorite part of therapy now is learning how to get rid of irrational fears. He can come up with tons of examples of irrational fears and he seems firm in the knowledge that each of them will not happen. He is excited to try it out for real. Maybe bedtime will give us a chance, but more than likely bedtime will be smooth sailing and I will have to come up with an outside challenge for him to test his new skills on. That is one responsibility that I am more than happy to take on!

Xanthe and Tahni spent the afternoon playing. Their new found closeness kept the usual arguments at bay. I stayed out of their way for awhile, but eventually the fun was too hard to resist. We ended up playing outside until dinner time.

Just as I suspected, bedtime was a breeze. After an hour of therapy practice, we were all relaxed and sleepy. I didn't want to head of to bed yet though, because I wanted to celebrate. I was proud of our progress. I invited them to cuddle with me on the sofa and I told them a bedtime story. It felt just like old times, times when they were younger, times before our lives were touched with this illness. By "happily ever after" they were both fast asleep. I lingered for a few minutes on the couch enjoying the moment before I ushered them off to bed.

THURSDAY OCTOBER 10TH

~ We went to see the therapist today. He was impressed with the progress we had made. He also praised Tahni's involvement. He pointed out that, not only was this involvement good for Xanthe's success, but that Tahni was gaining a great skill from it also. I hadn't thought of that angle before.

He then watched Xanthe and me practice our techniques and offered me advice on how to improve on them. The best part was that he agreed that it was working. Now he wants us to try a real life situation to see how Xanthe reacts in it. Obviously going to school is not a practical test, so I need to come up with something similar in stress level. I am thinking that I will have him spend the night with my mom. This is something he has not been able to do since last January.

After the session we picked up Tahni, then went out to eat to celebrate our success. Both kids wanted to go to a real restaurant, not a fast food joint, to celebrate. After we ordered, Xanthe launched into an animated monologue about the therapist visit and his words of praise. At first I was caught up in Xanthe's story, but soon I turned to stare at Tahni. I had to catch my breath when I looked into her eyes. She was staring at Xanthe with the same look of pride I bestowed on both of them. If you only saw her eyes at that moment, you might mistake her for the mom. My heart swelled with love and pride. I may have done a million things wrong up until now, but this moment proved to me that I must have done at least one thing right. Both of my children were happy, loving and empathetic. Not to shabby for twelve years worth of work!

FRIDAY OCTOBER 11TH

~ Today is the day that Xanthe will go stay with my mom. He seems very calm about the whole thing. After discussing it last night, it was decided that Tahni would stay also. Mom and I agreed that it was best to take baby steps on this one.

I woke him up around eight, we had a quick breakfast then we started our school lessons. Xanthe was very relaxed and focused through it all. He even spelled every one of his spelling words correctly!

After lunch we worked on his therapy. I incorporated a few of the changes that the therapist had suggested and we had great results. I can tell when we start now that he needs less instruction and that some techniques are becoming habit. He now breathes correctly without me having to mention it. I can also tell that his anxiety level is lessening as we proceed. Things are looking up.

I took Xanthe and Tahni to my mom's around six, stayed to eat dinner with them and then left. On the drive home I kept thinking that she would call me to turn around. All night I resisted the urge to call and check on him. Finally, at about midnight (when the phone still hadn't rung) I went to bed. I couldn't sleep though. In the dark and quiet room there was nothing to take my mind off the numerous what ifs invading my head. I gave up around one and quietly slipped into the living room to watch TV. My stomach hurt and I was nervous. Sometimes it is so hard to let go!

SATURDAY OCTOBER 12TH

~ Well Xanthe made it all night. I woke up at 9am and immediately called my mom. They had had a great evening. Throughout all the games and conversations, his anxiety stayed at bay. By bedtime, Xanthe was a little nervous and not at all ready to try to go to sleep. Tahni agreed to stay up with him and they watched TV, played board games and talked. Eventually, Tahni suggested that he try his techniques. He did this without her help and soon fell asleep on the sofa. Even better, he slept all night. When I asked him about it later, he exclaimed, "That therapy stuff really works!"

On the drive home, we talked about his experience. He did admit to being afraid and he agreed that it helped to have Tahni around. I think maybe next time we will try it without her. But for now I am ecstatic. He faced his first challenge and he came through with flying colors. I hope he is as proud of himself as I am. He deserves a round of applause!

Our evening went well. Chris was in a good mood since we had an evening to ourselves. The kids were relaxed and enjoying Chris' good humor. I was just thankful that it was all working out. Even the dogs seemed unusually happy.

Before bed, I prepared to practice our techniques, but Xanthe wanted to try them alone again. He wandered into the other room to have a little more quiet and I tensely waited his return. Twenty minutes later he flopped down next to me on the sofa, radiant and relaxed. I turned to hug him and he whispered in my ear, "I think I might be getting better Momma, it's all easier than before."

It took all the control I possessed not to break down and cry in front of him. These were words I had waited twelve long years to hear. Words that had the power to change our lives.

Bedtime was a breeze and I was actually able to relax. Instead of worries or concerns, my mind was filled with happiness and plans for a brighter future. It was a nice change of pace, and I fought sleep to make it last.

SUNDAY OCTOBER 13ᵀᴴ

~ I called my mom today to discuss her night with Xanthe. I wanted to make sure I hadn't missed anything. She only had great things to say about the evening. She was impressed with how well he reacted to her going to bed before him and she was equally impressed with Tahni's calming skills. She totally understood what a big step the night had been for him. She was even excited to try it again. That last idea got us talking. For years we had been discussing a short trip to Tennessee to see Roger, but of course the timing was never right. Mom was wondering if Xanthe would be capable of making the trip over Thanksgiving. I agreed to give it some thought, but it was too much for me to think about now, let alone Xanthe. I have to admit that the idea intrigued me though. It would be so awesome for Xanthe and Tahni to take a trip with their grandma. It is just the sort of thing "normal" kids do that they have been missing out on. Thanksgiving might be too soon, but the idea is worth considering. And who knows maybe he could make it and if not… well, I guess I could find a way to enjoy a late night emergency trip to Tennessee to rescue my son. Obviously, stranger things have happened!

After dinner I broached the subject of a trip to the kids. Both were immediately excited. Maybe I am the only one not sure of the idea. Xanthe was pretty positive that he could make it and Tahni seemed to agree. I think I will discuss it with his therapist. If he likes the idea, then I will be out numbered.

Unfortunately, bedtime was rough again. I guess some back sliding is to be expected, but it scared me. Xanthe was first afraid and then depressed when his techniques didn't work. This spiraled into an evening of self-doubt. As we sat together and tried to weather his bad mood, I was shaken to the core with feelings from past nights. I prayed that this was not the start of worse times. Infomercials ended up being our saving grace and we both fell asleep in front of the TV.

TUESDAY OCTOBER 15TH

~ To my great relief Xanthe woke up in a good mood today. It seems that I over reacted to our one rough night. Old habits die hard. This was not the beginning of the end after all, just a small set-back, an opportunity to try out our skills. I guess I failed the test, but at least I learned from it. Hopefully, next time I will react more calmly, and see the situation for what it really is- one night.

Tahni went off to school today a happy child and Chris and Xanthe went four-wheeling, since Chris had the day off. Did I sit around and wallow in self-pity? No! Partly because the stress from testing was over and partly because of my realization over the kitchen sink, I enjoyed the entire day. I even managed to rationalize my mistake from last night and chalk it up to experience without letting it get me down. I cleaned the house. I watched tons of cooking and house decorating shows. I made myself a real lunch, not one that comes in a pop can! and I enjoyed the moment. By dinner time I was proud of myself. I guess Xanthe is not the only one to benefit from some positive self-talk. Sometimes we all need to rewrite how we think about our lives. Too bad it took me twelve years to realize it.

Our evening went beautifully. Tahni was excited about her upcoming birthday and Xanthe was worn out from riding. After he showered he announced that he was going to bed. Alone? No way! But he did. Of course he went to lie down in my room, but he fell asleep without me beside him. I think this might be our biggest accomplishment yet!

WEDNESDAY OCTOBER 16TH

~ Xanthe slept all night last night and so did I. What a wonderful surprise! I felt good today and I think Xanthe did too! Even Chris was excited about the new development. Seeing real results has turned Chris around in his thoughts on therapy. He's even starting to believe we might have beaten this thing.

During our home schooling session, I watched Xanthe as he completed a rather tough math worksheet. With such intense concentration on his face, he looked so grown up. There was a confidence in his eyes that is usually hidden by fear. It was great to see him like that. At one point he looked up and caught me staring at him. His face changed back to that of my little boy as he said, "Thanks for everything mom. I love you!" Could any mother ask for more?

Since Xanthe seemed relaxed and last night had gone well, I broached the subject of Monday night with him. I explained my thoughts on the evening and asked him about his. He admitted to being freaked out by the set back, but thought that he could overcome it. I was excited by his mature outlook. We discussed some possible reasons for why the techniques failed and we brain-stormed for ways to handle the situation next time. I was nervous about bringing the topic up, but I feel better now. I think we needed to get it out in the open and work through it together. I know I feel better prepared now. I hope he does too.

Thankfully, bedtime went well again. Xanthe wasn't nervous or sad. Maybe Monday night was just a carry over from his night with my mom. Or maybe we are just destined to have rough nights. Either way, we made it. Let's hope he sleeps all night. I actually enjoyed my last eight uninterrupted hours and I wouldn't mind getting them again tonight.

MONDAY OCTOBER 21ST

~ Drum roll please...DA DA DA DAT TA DA... The test results are in! And boy, are they long. And the winners in the illness category are... Generalized Anxiety Disorder, Severe Separation Anxiety Disorder, School Phobia, Thought Disorder, ADHD and Bipolar II Disorder. What does it all mean? Funny you should ask. It means we are now, and have been for sometime, doing the right therapies. The recommended therapy includes Systematic Desensitizing Training (that would be the electrified chair story), Cognitive Therapy to challenge negative thoughts (positive self-talk) and special education classes at school (well, this one will have to wait!).

As for medication recommendations, we are on the right track there also. The Celexa will help with both anxiety disorders. We are increasing the dosage though. The Lamictal and Lithium will help with the bipolar disorder. We may need to tweak with those dosages as time goes on. We need to add back in the Adderall for ADHD, but not until his anxiety is under control and there are no other medications for the school phobia or thought disorder. The Celexa will help a little with school, but mostly therapy will be our answer for these two conditions. The only other addition is a medication to induce sleep, Trazadone. This will help shut off his busy mind and ease him into sleep each night. Yea, no more Benadryl.

After the medication and therapy recommendations, we discussed her findings. It was both scary and comforting to hear the symptoms laid out. On one hand, the exact words, spoken out loud scared me with their degree of seriousness and hostility. On the other hand, it was comforting to know that these symptoms were recognized by someone else and I wasn't crazy.

The results of the TAT test (Thematic Apperception Test) were the scariest. This was the test with the black and white pictures. His stories suggested high levels of anxiety and possible paranoia. Their content included references to being poisoned and being shot and suggested feelings of guilt, betrayal, deceit and fear.

As I hung up the phone with the psychologist, my only thought was, "Great, it's finally over." I wasn't surprised with the diagnosis and I wasn't afraid of the suggested therapy. It was all something I had already become quite comfortable with. I do not even have to question were we go from here. Fortunately for us, we are already well on our way.

EPILOGUE

Ever since we received the test results, life has gotten better and better for us. It is nice to have a firm diagnosis now, but I find that I am not putting as much stock into it as I thought I would. Numerous times over the years we have been given a "firm diagnosis," but it has never really made a big difference. The big change came with the right therapy. Of course, you need a diagnosis to design the therapy plan, but as you can see from our story, every once in a while the plan precedes the diagnosis and it turns out just fine.

Throughout the years, every professional we have seen has stressed the importance of therapy, but unfortunately they never stressed the importance of the *right* therapy. We wasted a lot of years doing the wrong thing. The knowledge we have acquired in the last few months coupled with the right medication combination leads me to believe we may have this thing beat. We just have to keep in mind what we have been through and how far we have come. We have had worse days in the past, and we will have bad days in the future just like everyone else, but we will know that that is just what they are...bad days. We now have faith that tomorrow can be better. The two medications that we added and the two that we dropped seem to have made a big difference. And both therapies are working wonders. It is great to have concrete family therapy each week and not just an hour of pointless talk. And the habit changing therapy is a gift from God. Now when something small happens that used to make him freak out, I cringe and wait, but nothing happens. By *habit* he just overcomes it. I do not think that he even realizes it happens.

And the changes we have made as a family seem to be complimenting it all as well. Will life always be better and easier? Probably not. Will we ever see the day that Xanthe is symptom free? Who knows? We still have many years of hard work ahead of us. At anytime, Xanthe's body chemistry could change and his medication combination could stop working. Or something could change in his life that would cause him to relapse. But if and when that happens, we will be better prepared this time. We will know that there is a light at the end of the tunnel because we have seen it once before.

People ask me now if I have any regrets or if I would change anything. At first I was quick to answer that question. I used to think that I would change a lot. That I would ask that this illness never even touch our family. But now I am not so sure. These years of suffering and confusion actually turned out to be a gift in a strange way. It brought us closer together as a family. We learned to rely on each other. We learned that at even the worst times, the times that we were mad or frustrated or hurtful, we still had people that loved us. We also learned that families forgive, love and grow together. Bad things are going to happen to everyone. We now have the knowledge that no matter what "bad things" come our way we can handle them together. This entire ordeal has made us stronger, wiser and in the end happier than I thought we could ever be. We appreciate the good times more. We live each day as if it's a gift. And that is really what it is! Our lives are a gift. It is up to each of us how we use that gift. Because of what we have lived through and learned, we mostly use our gifts wisely.

Just the other day life took a fleeting turn for the worse and how we handled it proved to me that we would be just fine. Xanthe had a flash of his old anxiety; he was frightened and anxious at bedtime because he had seen an advertisement for a scary Halloween movie. He was convinced that what happened to those people could happen to us. Instead of getting upset or expecting the worse, I lay down next to him and we went through some of the various techniques we had learned. Within an hour he was fast asleep and he slept through the night. Tahni had a terrible day at school because she had received a bad grade on a paper and had to stay inside for recess because she was talking in the line. Chris and I had bounced a check to the mortgage company. Instead of all of us retreating to ourselves, eating a silent dinner and lashing out over the smallest offense, we tried hard to make each other laugh. Xanthe made a joke about Tahni at least *going* to school, Tahni teased Xanthe about his mean, strict teacher (me!) and Chris asked us how much money we thought he could make as a male stripper to cover the mortgage check. That last idea made us laugh so hard we cried. After we had all stopped laughing, I just sat there and stared at the faces of my family. I was suddenly overcome by how much I loved them and how lucky we were to be a family. I can honestly say that I would do everything all over again just to have that one moment. Miracles do happen. I live one everyday.

IMPORTANT STEPS AND TREATMENTS

A Full Medical Work-up- It is highly important to have a full medical work-up preformed by your doctor before beginning any medications or therapy. Many times there are underlying medical conditions or diseases that could be causing the psychological symptoms. Not only do these need to be ruled out first, but the results from all the blood work, electrocardiograms and other assorted tests will aid in choosing medications and in weighing their risks.

Psychological Testing- These tests, which include personality testing, anxiety testing and symptom analysis testing are extremely important in identifying the actual symptoms and underlying causes. The condition that a person originally seeks help for does not usually turn out to be the major illness that the person is suffering from. In order to treat a person successfully, the doctor needs to identify and treat the actual illness, not just improve the symptoms it causes.

Behavioral/ Cognitive Therapy- While regular "talk" therapy is important and useful, behavioral therapy can prove to be the key in controlling a person's symptoms. This type of therapy concentrates on teaching a person to relearn their reactions to different stimuli and situations. With this therapy, a person can learn to control their reactions and become free from the anxiety and fear that certain situations bring on.

Family Therapy- While some insurance companies do not cover this type of therapy it is well worth looking into. This therapy revolves around treating the entire family, not just the individual with the symptoms. Through this therapy, each family member learns to cope with what is going on in the house and they learn ways to help, ways to relieve their own frustrations and ways to live in harmony. This type of therapy holds families together in the face of crisis.

Relaxation techniques- Of course, there is no substitute for professional therapy, but you can work on helping yourself or your loved one at home. These techniques can be used at home to practice relaxation, to stop the progression of anxiety and to help each family member reduce stress. These techniques include yoga, meditation, deep breathing, aromatherapy, music therapy, color therapy, and massage. While there are books available on all of these topics, the best thing to do is to discuss the existence of these techniques with your doctor, see which ones he suggests for you and then buy the books that outline the techniques for your use at home.

What follows is a small list of professional therapy exercises that we found helpful. Take this list with you to your next doctor appointment and use it as a starting point to open a discussion with your doctor about what you can be doing at home to improve your situation:

Intensity of Distress Scale
The Eye-Movement Technique
Tips for Relaxation Training
Cognitive Problem Solving
Correcting Irrational Self-talk
Deep Breathing Exercises

RESOURCES

Gardener, James M.D., and Arthur H. Bell, Ph.D.. Overcoming Anxiety, Panic and Depression. New Jersey: The Career press, Inc., 2000.

Papolos, Demitri M.D., and Janice Papolos. The Bipolar Child. New York: Broadway Books, 1999

Smyth, Larry D. Ph.D.. Client's Manual for the Cognitive-Behavioral Treatment of Anxiety Disorders. Maryland: RTR Publishing Company, 1999

Wolpe, Joseph M.D., and David Wolpe. Our Useless Fears. Boston: Houghton Mifflin Company, 1981.

Printed in the United Kingdom
by Lightning Source UK Ltd.
108144UKS00001B/32